How to acquire the

POWER OF

FINANCIAL

INDEPENDENCE

ANDREW JAMES McLEAN

ISBN 0-930648-03-X

Title Code #1144

Printed in the United States of America
First printing...November 1978

Additional copies available direct from the publisher at $6.95 plus 60¢ postage and handling. Mail to JWP Development, PO Box 2531, Culver City, CA 90230.

Published by
JWP Development
The "How-to" publishers
PO Box 2531, Culver City, CA 90230

Other titles by Andrew James McLean

HOW TO MANAGE REAL ESTATE PROFITABLY

THE POWER OF REAL ESTATE and how to acquire it in your spare time.

TABLE OF CONTENTS . . . BOOK I

TABLE OF CONTENTS . . . BOOK II

INTRODUCTION

The most exciting business in the entire universe is about to unfold before you. To make it even more appealing, I have incorporated two phases of it into separate volumes just to be sure of making the entire book as valuable to you as I could deem possible.

Book I is a thorough step-by-step guide to acquiring financial independence by investing in real estate in your spare time. Do not confuse me with others who have written large volumes on the subject. I pride myself in guiding you precisely, in a condensed, yet thorough form. Some of the principles have been rather basic over the past fifty years, but I add a wrinkle here and a twist there making them easier to understand with a well formulated plan.

Book II is, without a doubt, the greatest business in the entire universe. Why is it so great? Because you can begin at home during your spare time. It is the direct reply business and it doesn't require large amounts of capital to get started. In more common terms, it is the mail order business, and from it you can create a national, or even a world-wide business almost over night. And I'm going to show you how. From a complete business set-up to how to write, how to sell and advertise. I have included a complete list of ideas to start with. With some ingenuity on your part we can develop almost anything with enterprising uniqueness. I plan to show you how to develop just about any form of information, product or service, sell it, and make a good future for yourself doing it.

Fortunes and financial independence are not made by drudging away unconsciously in the employ of someone else, but by having the knowledge of how fortunes are made, and then putting this knowledge to practical use. The knowledge is forthcoming in what you are about to read; putting it to practical use will be up to you.

You don't need experience, money, education, or luck. What you do need is a little motivation and some determination. With those ingredients I am going to turn you on to acquiring financial independence in various forms of businesses that anyone can develop in their spare time, out of their own home; and you won't even have to quit your present job.

Possibly you're tired of working for less than you're really worth...or working in a field you no longer enjoy? Wouldn't you enjoy financial freedom and the time to do all those things you've always wanted to do? Then now is the time for me to turn you on because this guidebook was expressly written for you.

If you have a thirst for financial independence, if you desire a business of your own, or if you're looking for that professional career which will make you the person you've always dreamed of becoming...then this guidebook was written for and is dedicated to you.

BOOK I

WHY REAL ESTATE?

Land is the basis of a nation's wealth. Its natural resources and productive facilities are derived from it. And as the world has developed itself into fortresses of capitalism and socialism, empires and republics, "haves" and "have-nots", nations continue to fight tragic wars over it, and millions have died for it, and most millionaires are made from it.

Besides the dream of everyone to own his own home, real estate is needed by all in some form or another. Everyone must have a place to live; either as a guest at a hotel, or renting a home or a summer estate. As a tenant he pays the owner a rent that compensates for his investment, plus a suitable amount for taxes and maintenance. This compensation is prevalent in every form of land occupation, whether the tenant conducts a local grocery store, a huge department emporium, or a manufacturing facility. And when a tenant makes payment to the possessor for the use of the land and improvements, it is always an expense to the tenant, while it is income to the landlord.

Unlike other assets, land cannot be manufactured at will. It is basically indestructible, and as populations continue to expand, the demand for land becomes insatiable. From the beginning of time, men have been acquiring property, trading it, improving it, farming it, and selling it to fellow landlords. Why real estate as a basis for wealth? Because for more than fifty years real estate has endured as the surest and safest form of investment, offering a return of 50 to 100% and more on invested capital annually. Even during the depression when all forms of assets were devalued substantially, owners of land were hurt the least.

Other forms of investment, like the stock market, do not offer the leverage, the tax advantage, nor the profit and safety of real estate. Broad fluctuations of stock prices often occur in market conditions which are entirely unpredictable and uncontrollable by the investor. Experienced stock traders often can make money in the securities market, but for the average investor, investing in stocks is a very risky gamble.

Savings accounts are an ideal place to store cash for the future purchase of real estate. Other than that, they merely return enough to contend with inflation, if you're lucky. And what about the taxes you pay on your dividends?

Gold and silver experience erratic up and down price movement, as does the stock market. On top of the risk involved, you have to store and protect your hoards of pretty metal.

Vacant land is good only if you can afford to have your capital tied up waiting for civilization to reach your door step. Unlike improved property, which can be rented and depreciated, vacant land is quite speculative and requires a lot of patience and plenty of "bread".

NOW IS THE TIME TO START

If you do not already own your own home, or any other real estate, it is time to prepare for your first purchase. Your first home will allow you a base of operations and give you an established credit rating for future loans. It may become essential for you to borrow against equity you might have acquired in your existing home to begin financing future investments.

In case you don't have the necessary cash for a down payment for your first purchase, you have a number of alternatives available. You can begin saving for it, or you can borrow the down payment. Borrowing the down payment is a little riskier because you will have to make monthly payments on your new purchase, as well as on the loan for the down payment. Borrowing a down payment was how I bought my second home and if you are to be successful in real estate, it is essential you learn how to borrow money. Borrowing money to invest in real estate is a very sound venture, and you must not be overly timid. As you will see, the least amount of cash you invest in real estate, the more profitable it will be for you. If you have the means to make the total monthly payments...by all means borrow.

I have never met anyone who made a fortune in real estate by waiting for the right time to buy. Interest rates will go up and down, and the real estate market will experience short slowing and booming trends, but property values will never be less than they are right now...and the longer you wait...the more it will cost you.

Don't be timid about borrowing money! Don't look at it as if you're going into debt. What you're actually doing is becoming partners with the bank, only you don't have to split the profits. I cannot stress this point enough; if you are reluctant to borrow money to purchase properties, you will not be a successful real estate investor.

Your first major objective in your overall strategy of acquiring the Power of Financial Independence is to acquire $200,000 in net worth. This amount will be represented by $200,000 in equities in your future purchases. To attain this objective, you can utilize any one of the following methods:

✦ The easiest method is to already have on hand a substantial amount of excess cash, which can be used for a down payment. If this is the case, then you will be much further ahead and can expand faster than those who do not. A substantial amount would be a minimum of approximately $10,000 which you could immediately put down on a property once you locate it.

✦ The second method involves owning your own home, but having no cash for a down payment. You probably have some equity build-up in your existing home, which you can borrow against for a long term loan and use the proceeds of the loan to buy a second property.

✦ You can also start your investment program by borrowing from relatives. It may be possible to work out a deal where you pay interest on the loan only at a reasonable rate for a lengthy term from your understanding kin-folk.

✦ With good credit and references, you can begin your quest for financial independence by borrowing from a bank. I used this method on my second property when I needed $7,500 down and only had $1,500 of my own. In fact, I borrowed the remaining $6,000 I needed from two banks. It was a very profitable situation when I later sold the property and paid everyone off.

RICHES ARE ATTAINED
FROM BORROWED MONEY

General Motors, Rockefeller, and large real estate operators alike, acquire millions in assets without putting up a nickel of their own money. Many top bank executives could easily pay cash for a new home, but only put a small down payment towards the purchases and borrow the balance over an extended period of time. The reason, which you might already know, is *leverage;* ie, using borrowed money to control assets. The less cash you invest in a property and the more you borrow to purchase it, the more leverage you are using. Maximum leverage is 100% financing with no money of your own to control the property.

As you will soon see, leverage buying allows a much higher rate of return on your invested capital than using 100% cash down without any loans. The main reason why this occurs is because you're borrowing money at one interest rate, then reinvesting it at a higher rate.

An example of why we grow rich on borrowed money can be seen from my first investment. My initial purchase was a single family residence located in Lansing, Michigan. It was a two story, three bedroom (Archie Bunker type), "fixer-upper", built in 1937, purchased for $13,400 on a 7% land contract with $1,500 down. It needed interior and exterior paint, plus new interior wiring to conform to local building codes.

I did the painting myself and contracted the electrical work out at $400. After finishing all the refurbishment, I moved furniture in, which was a gift from my grandmother, and rented out the house to three bachelors for a total of $240 a month. My total monthly payment, including principal and interest on the loan, taxes, and insurance, was $138 a month. This left a net monthly profit of $102. ($240 less $138 is $102). My total cash outlay so far was $1,500 down payment, $400 for electrical work and $100 for paint and materials, or a total of $2,000.

To figure an annual return on investment, we take the $102 monthly net profit, multiply it by twelve months and divide by $2,000. (My initial cash outlay). The result ($102 x 12 equals $1224), divided by $2,000 equals 61.2% return on invested capital, and I haven't told you the best part yet. About a year later, I was able to sell this home for a handsome profit of $1,800. The initial 61.2% return was only generated while holding the property. Now we can figure total return on investment by adding profit made at the time of sale to the net profit made while holding. (I purposely omitted misc. expenses incurred at time of sale, and other small costs involved while holding the property, to show only a net figure to simplify my example.)

Allow me to portray the principles of leverage by comparing two methods of purchasing my first home. The first example will be using all cash to purchase. The second example we will use leverage.

USING ALL CASH

$13,400 cash purchase price
     500 cost of refurbishment
$13,900 total cash investment
$240 rent less $40 (taxes & ins) equals $200
$200 net per month x 12 equals $2400 annual net profit
plus $1800 profit at sale
$4200 total profit
$4200 divided by $13,900 (total cash investment) equals 30.2%
30.2% equals total return on investment using all cash.

USING LEVERAGE

$13,400 purchase price
  1,500 down payment
     500 cost of refurbishment
 $2,000 total cash investment
$240 rent less $138 (loan payment, taxes & ins.) equals $102
$102 x 12 equals $1,224 annual profit
plus $1,800 profit at sale
$3,024 total profit
$3,024 divided by $2000 (total cash investment) equals 151.2%
151.2% equals total return on investment using leverage.

Note that using leverage we have over five times the total return that we have using all cash. (151.2% versus 30.2%). Leverage will always show a higher rate of return than an all cash investment, because you are profiting from a return on borrowed money while only having a small amount of your own money controlling the property.

PREPARATION FOR ACTION

Dreams...or perhaps a dream beyond your wildest dream. Dreaming is fine; we all do it, some more than others, but dreams are basically worthless, unless they are transposed into action that eventually becomes a reality. The basic difference between the "haves" and the "have-nots" is that the have-nots do plenty of dreaming, but the haves convert their dreams into reality by working at a well developed plan.

Rome wasn't built in a day, nor was the empire of Sears and Roebuck or the vast chain of Hilton hotels, or whatever large conglomeration of corporations you think of as being successful. Each of those successful endeavors began with a dream followed by careful planning, then investment and continued reinvestment.

No matter what type of successful business we use as an example, it began with a dream that was followed by preconceived action that came from a well devised plan.

ELIMINATE NEGATIVE THINKING

Did you ever wonder why there are four times as many losers as there are winners at almost everything in life? In Las Vegas, in the sales force at a large corporation, or in the entire population of the United States, only a small percentage have absolute wealth and financial independence.

The majority of those who frequent Las Vegas go with the attitude that they will lose what they take with them...and that they will, especially if they retain that losing attitude. With a large corporation, statistical results have proven that 5% of the sales force actually produce 80% of all the sales. And, out of the two hundred million plus population of the United States, where more millionaires reside than in any other country, yet these prosperous few merely consist of only a small percentage of the total people.

The reason is essentially too much negative thinking; or in other words, an unwillingness to accentuate the positive. If one doesn't attempt something, an endeavor, a business, or whatever, he doesn't have a chance to succeed. True, some have tried and failed, but if they continue to try, eventually they will triumph.

You can't be stuck the rest of your life looking back at past mistakes, regretting lost opportunities, wishing you had invested in this or that. You have to accentuate the positive, eliminate the negative and begin trying...because today is the first day of the rest of your life. Yesterday is gone, with all its foolish mistakes and can never return.

When you say you can't, what you're really saying is: you won't. And if you won't even try, absolutely nothing will ever happen. But if you try, and then try again, you will eventually succeed.

People react to the attitude you portray. Try playing catch with a friend; you'll be surprised how often your friend will quit playing with you when you stop making an effort to catch what he throws. People will react to you with a pleasant smile and response when you show an enthusiastic smile, but try an ugly sneer and see what their response is.

A dear friend of mine, Rick Hamilton, who I personally witnessed positive thinking catapault him into riches, success, and a rewarding career. It all began when he was laid off from a cushey sales position with a large food company, which had ceased doing business on the West Coast. Previously, Rick had worked for the Mariott Hotel for next to nothing managing a restaurant with the hotel after graduating from college. His dream in life was to have enough income to allow him to play golf five days a week, without working. He really hated work and obviously loved golf. He decided to get his real estate license and begin a career selling residential real estate.

Rick's real estate broker provided him with various training and motivational tapes. When I'd visit him at home, he would be nestled back in a lounge chair listening to tape after tape telling him what was required to make $30,000 selling real estate his first year in the business. In essence, the tapes were saying, "In order to list homes for sale, you must begin cold, calling your potential clients asking them if you can sell their home for them. For every 100 people you talk to, you will make a listing appointment with two and you will actually list for sale one out of every two appointments. Each home you list will represent $3,000 in sales commissions . Therefore, to make $30,000 or more, you must list approximately one house a month, or cold call 100 people per month".

I was amazed because I had never seen him so motivated before. He could actually see the handwriting on the wall. By making $30,000 a year, he could afford to invest in the booming California real estate market which would even add more to his income and could eventually result in his financial independence.

This, of course would allow him to spend most of his time out on the golf course.

Today, two and a half years after watching him listen to those tapes, Rick is worth in excess of $200,000. His first year in the business he made $32,000 and his second year he made $50,000. Plus, he continued to invest all his excess income in real estate. Today he claims he will fully retire in two more years to play golf full time. Rick is only thirty years old. He will be completely self made; he didn't inherit a dime but started two years ago with nothing but positive thoughts from motivating tapes and a goal.

ESTABLISHING GOALS

Besides having positive thoughts, one must set goals in order to have targets to aim for. Your overall objective of financial independence is fine, but you need preliminary goals to work towards in order to reach your ultimate goal. Don't establish goals which may be too difficult to attain at first.

As an example, to reach financial independence in real estate, one must begin purchasing one property at a time. In order to purchase the first property, a down payment is required. Therefore, your first goal will be to acquire the initial down payment. Then your second objective will be to locate and purchase your first property. Your third goal will be to save for the down payment on your next purchases, and so on. Reaching each of these goals will gradually lead you to your ultimate goal of financial independence.

Let's assume you do not have any existing savings to speak of; so in order to start investing, you will need to save a down payment. You must begin immediately to set aside a minimum of 10% of your gross earnings, and you must not spend this savings for any reason whatsoever. Your savings will become your capital and must never be touched, except for investment in real estate.

Typically, most Americans will save for various depreciating assets, such as an expensive sportscar, a camper, a boat or a vacation, continually spending, never investing, and eventually never really having anything except a few depreciating toys laying around. Later on, once you reach your ultimate objective, you can begin enjoying your money on these toys, but until then you must live somewhat frugally. It's the only way you can become successful and attain complete financial independence.

Many will claim they cannot save any money. If you feel this way, evaluate your paycheck and see where your money is going. If you're eating steak, start eating hamburger. If you're driving a Caddy, trade it for a Chevy. If you're going out to dinner two or three times a week, make it once a week. There are plenty of areas where you can budget your money and save a minimum of 10%.

If you can save more than 10%, you're that much farther ahead. The sooner you set aside enough savings for your first down payment, the faster you will obtain your final objective.

The importance of savings as the initial step to eventual financial independence cannot be underestimated. But obviously it is not that apparent to most men and women since many who look forward to wealth and success in their mid 20's, end up broke in their sixties. Tragic but true, statistics show that of 100 people taken randomly at the age of 25, all looking forward to a rewarding future, after a lifetime of working, only one of the 100 will truly be rich, 5 will be somewhat financially independent, 33 will have died of various causes, 6 will still be working, and 55 of the original 100 will be broke. How sad and mind-boggling in a country so rich with opportunity!

Part of the reason for this mediocricy and failure is the inability to acquire what is known as capital. Capital begins with savings; people simply do not save to acquire the capital, which in turn can give them wealth when properly invested.

COMPOUNDING YOUR WAY TO WEALTH

The effects of compounding has a phenomenal effect on growth. It might be difficult to comprehend how phenomenal without giving you a good example. In Mark Haroldsen's book "How To Wake Up The Financial Genius Inside You", he uses an example of compounding one penny at 100% a day for 35 days. The starting result is over a third of a billion dollars accumulated on the thirty-fifth day. It may sound hard to believe at first until you realize that a penny is doubling in value everyday at 100% compounded interest, 1¢ to 2¢, 2 to 4, 4 to 8, etc. By the 16th day, one-cent has compounded in value to $652.80. Now that compounding has gone from one cent to in excess of six hundred dollars, the effects of compounding really begins to take a staggering effect as the next compounding results in over a thousand dollars.

Compounding at 100% is not really a practical figure to use, although it is very dramatic for the purposes of this example. In reality, I plan to work with you at a 15 to 25% compounding rate to develop your investment portfolio into a multi-million dollar estate. Some shrewd investors can compound their net worth annually at 100%. Often I have done so with certain individual properties, however 15-25% is a good rate to work from as an all around conservative average range of compounding and growth.

Virtually, all self-made millionaires have compounded their original worth into wealth using various different vehicles of investment. It is basically starting with a base of investment capital, then investing it, making the initial investment appreciate while receiving interest on that investment, and receiving interest on the gains from the investment.

On the following pages I have set up an investment schedule based on an initial investment base of $10,000, then a continued rate of savings of $3,000 annually every year for the first five years after the initial $10,000 is attained. The initial $10,000 will be invested in $67,000 worth of real estate which will appreciate on the average of 15% a year. $67,000 in real estate was arrived at by using $10,000 as a down payment of 15% to purchase $67,000 gross value of real estate.

INVESTMENT PROGRAM

Starting with an initial capital base of $10,000, then saving $3,000 a year to continue investing in real estate. The initial savings of $10,000 will buy $67,000 worth of real estate as the $10,000 represents an average 15% down payment. In the following five years an additional $3,000 per year will be saved to purchase an additional $20,000 worth of real estate. After every five year period, you will increase your savings to invest by $3,000. At the end of each year, we apply 15% appreciation to real estate already acquired, then add each years additional purchase to the accumulated total.

Explanations of the following calculations:

After saving $10,000, the first year you purchase $67,000 in real estate. You now have $10,000 used as a 15% down payment invested in $67,000 gross value of real estate.

$67,000 gross value in real estate is now multiplied by a 15% appreciation factor, and the accumulated value is now worth $77,050. By the end of the second year you have saved an additional $3,000 and used that to invest in an additional $20,000 worth of real estate. At the end of the second year, you add the additional $20,000 to the first year gross value in real estate owned ($77,050) and the result at the end of the second year is a total gross value in real estate of $97,050. This similar process continues to the 12th year at which time you have acquired in excess of one-million dollars in gross value of real estate.

$67,000 real estate acquired, end of first year.
  x1.15 15% appreciation factor
 77,050
+20,000 real estate acquired during second year
 97,050 total real estate owned, end of second year.
  x1.15
111,608
+20,000
131,608 total real estate owned, end of third year.
  x1.15
151,349
+20,000
171,349 total real estate owned, end of fourth year.
  x1.15
197,051

```
 +20,000
 217,051  total real estate owned, end of fifth year.
   x1.15
 249,609
 +40,000  At this point, you increase down payment in-
 289,609  vestment annually from $3,000 per year to
          $6,000 per year, which increases real estate
 289,609  owned from $20,000 to $40,000 per year.
   x1.15
 333,050
 +40,000
 373,050  total real estate owned, end of seventh year.
   x1.15
 429,008
 +40,000
 469,008  total real estate owned, end of eighth year.
   x1.15
 539,359
 +40,000
 579,359  total real estate owned, end of ninth year.
   x1.15
 666,263
 +40,000
 706,263  total real estate owned, end of tenth year.
   x1.15
 812,202
  60,000  At this point, you again increase down pay-
 872,202  ment annually from $6,000 to 9,000 annually,
          which will increase real estate acquired each
          year to $60,000 from $40,000.
 872,202  total real estate owned, end of eleventh year.
   x1.15
$1,003,032
  60,000
```

$1,063,032 total real estate owned, end of twelve years. At the end of twelve years you will have accumulated in excess of one-million dollars in real estate owned. Your total net worth, or equity position, will be in excess of $200,000. With a 15% continued appreciation factor, you will continue to earn over $150,000 in appreciation annually on the one million plus in real estate holdings.

Please note that at the end of each five year period of investment program you increase investment monies by $3,000. Because five years of continued investment and appreciation, it will be easier to either save or borrow this additional amount to further increase your purchasing power as your net worth and total income will have increased substantially over the first year you began investing.

Furthermore, just because you have reached a pinnacle of over one million in real estate by the end of the 12th year doesn't mean you have to stop there. Although this objective will definitely allow you financial independence. To further invest at the same pace will make you a sure-fire millionaire after a conscientious effort during the first twelve years.

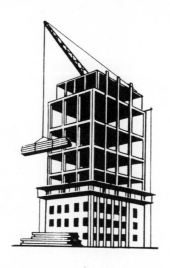

INFLATION AND APPRECIATION

Understanding inflation, allowing it to be your ally and not your enemy, can help you build your empire of financial independence. The figures I used in the preceeding example may sound low in today's skyrocketing real estate market. However, you must realize that seven years ago I was paying a high price relative to the ten years before I purchased that particular property. According to the U.S. Commerce Department, a home priced at $24,000 in 1966 today costs in excess of $53,000. That is over a 100% increase!

Rising prices caused by inflation certainly are a problem for fixed wage consumers. But to the real estate investor, inflation is an added windfall. Real estate historically has been extremely sensitive to inflation. While inflation may average 5 to 8% per year, real estate values have increased 10 to 15% over the same period.

Everytime a plumber or electrician, carpenter or roofer receives a new contract for higher wages, the price of new homes goes up a little more. The fact that land to build new homes on is becoming scarcer everyday, helps add to the ever increasing prices of homes. And used homes will always follow the trail of spiraling prices of new construction.

You must begin anticipating both appreciation and inflation. You cannot look back and say "I could have bought that house ten years ago for $20,000 and today it's worth $60,000." You have to look at a potential purchase and figure what kind of profit you will realize in the future.

Here are some more figures to startle your thinking! The U.S. Department of Labor has compiled cost of living indexes which represent a sampling of 400 items, including food, clothing, health care, housing and transportation. Since 1974 through 1977, the cost of living index has increased 30.6%. That's an average of over 7.5% a year. Long range government planning is trying to maintain a 5% average cost of living increase year to year.

Sound startling? By the year 2000, new homes will be built by a carpenter who makes in excess of $129,000 a year. And, if you fly to New York during that year, you will be attended by a stewardess who makes in excess of $50,000 a year. Those are the projections of the U.S. Department of Labor statistics. They also project that by the year 2000 a job paying $25,000 a year today, will be paying $110,000, and minimum wages will attain a $19,000 a year level.

While the consumer price index is merely representative of a broad price range of overall products and services, the real estate market has experienced a much higher advance in prices over the same period.

I'm not trying to promote inflation, nor justify it. The fact is that it is here, and that it has been more rampant in the 1970's than in the past. A steady rate of inflation is often healthy for the real estate market. However, when inflation reaches a level in excess of 20%, as it did in certain areas of the U.S. during the late 1970's, you can always expect a short cooling off trend to follow, usually lasting six months to a year.

Even with zero rate of inflation, owning rental property is still very profitable. Buying and selling correctly, along with proper management of your estate, will allow you an excellent return on your investment. Inflation and appreciation just give you that added edge, or hedge, against inflation, which the ownership of other assets does not allow.

Inflation not only affects prices, they affect wages too. Don't forget about the stewardess on your future flight to New York who will be making in excess of $50,000 a year. You may say, "who will be able to afford the homes of the future?" Well, as the consumer price index soared 30.6% during the last four years, wage earners were able to get increases above 9% a year for the past two years.

Everyone today is talking about who can afford to buy a home. Well, last year there were more homes sold in the U.S. than in any other year. Those that are sitting around complaining about the record high prices of homes will have plenty to grumble about when those homes cost even more in the future. You know the people I'm talking about, the "I should have bought that years ago" type, who'll end up in their old age talking about all their past dreams that never came true...because they didn't act!

You must take the bull by the horns and face the reality that the house you find today, at today's record prices, will be worth plenty more tomorrow. There hasn't been a financial winner born who was a pessimist. You must be an optimist to be a winner. Awaiting for the crumbling of the market or a coming depression will keep you from tasting the fruits of success in real estate. All you will ever see are slight up and down price movements of the market. Real estate has not decreased in price since 1929, except for short cooling off periods, and there isn't any reason why it should be any different in the future.

WHERE & HOW TO BORROW MONEY

Lending institutions do not lend money on the basis of need; they lend on the ability to repay. The following material covered in this area will be the basic principles to guide you when it comes time to borrow money.

A. Update your credit, if it isn't current already.
B. Complete financial requirements of money needed, and how it will be paid back, must be put in written form before you borrow.
C. Prepare an accurate financial statement.
D. Always borrow the highest repayable amount, with the lowest possible payments, for the longest period of time.

When you apply to the source of your loan, have exact figures ready. If you want a home improvement loan for $5,000, a complete breakdown of what the improvements will be and how much they will cost have to be made.

The more money you borrow, the faster you can pyramid your investments. On each individual project, get the maximum loan possible. Seldom will you be able to borrow more than you can repay; however, try and keep monthly payments safely within your income. Lowest possible payments will enable you to have a larger monthly net income, which can be saved for future investment. And of course, if your credit is not up to date, your ability to acquire a loan will be hampered substantially.

When you have this data prepared, it's time to make a loan request. How you make your presentation can determine your success. Your request will require some salesmanship, because your purpose is really to "sell" the lender on lending you the money.

All your paperwork should be legible and organized, showing a complete picture of your financial plans. Personally contact the lender, and be dressed in businesslike attire. Be confident, and get to the point. The lender wants to know what the loan is for and how you will pay it back. Once you have told him, he will ask you to fill out a loan application. Once an agreement has been reached, it's time to leave. Say goodbye, you will be notified of the decision one way or the other.

Convincing the lender that your plans are sound, and that you will repay the loan, is your objective. Lenders are anxious to lend money; that's their business.

THE REAL ESTATE MONEY MARKET

Sources of money are almost unlimited; however, I plan to describe the conventional sources to enable you to understand basically how they function. I also include normal interest rates pertinent to the current money market.

Savings and loan associations primarily lend money on real estate using either a mortgage or a first deed of trust. (From this point on I strictly refer to mortgages to simplify the situation. Although a deed of trust is similar to a mortgage, technically it is quite different and I don't feel it is important for you to know the difference.) The type of loan acquired from a savings and loan, based on a mortgage, usually has the best terms, (lowest payment and interest rate, for the longest period). Duration of the loan can vary, but usually is between twenty and thirty years. Today there is a trend towards considering a forty year term, which would enable new home buyers more purchasing power by reducing monthly principal and interest payments. Current interest rates involving savings and loans have been fluctuating between 8.5% to 10.5%. One reason for lower rates than other sources is because of lower risk in real estate. The lender utilizes the property as collateral. Should the borrower default on the loan, the property is taken back through the act of foreclosure.

Banks, unlike savings and loans, basically make commercial loans; however, some home improvement money may be available. Commercial loans can involve signature loans with no collateral, or loans for business working capital using inventory of the business for security against default. Banks also sponsor Mastercharge and Bankamericard where instant money is available with the ease of a signature. Installment loans on boats and cars for three to four year terms are also popular with banks. A successful property owner will accomplish his commercial loan borrowing with signature alone, supported by the strength of his financial statement. Bank interest rates vary substantially, depending on the type of the loan and if any collateral is involved.

Credit unions are an invaluable source, should you be fortunate enough to belong to one. Credit unions pay their depositor's interest on savings accounts, plus a portion of year end profits.

They usually will lend on almost anything and tend to have a rather liberal policy. A friend of mine once borrowed $25,000 on his signature to use for a down payment on a large apartment building. Interest rates can vary from approximately 8% to 12%.

Finance companies usually lend for shorter terms and almost always charge the highest interest rates. Not only are you raked over the coals on interest rates, loan fees are also very costly. Rates can be as high as 18% on small loans and 12 to 15% on larger loans of $5,000 to $10,000. Normally, I would only borrow from finance companies as a last resort.

In the last few years many second mortgage home-loan-companies have developed, who confine their operations to lending money for a second mortgage on an existing home. If you have enough equity in a home, these companies will lend you money utilizing a second mortgage as security against default. Their interest rates are fairly reasonable, usually about 10%, with varying terms of three to ten years. However, they do charge large fees for writing the loan. These fees can run up to fifteen points (15% of $10,000 would equal $1,500) to initiate the loan.

FUNCTIONING OF THE MONEY MARKET

Lending institutions take in deposits which they pay interest on. These deposits are then loaned out, or invested in interest yielding securities of all types. Profit is made on the spread in interest rates paid on deposits and money loaned out to other customers. For example, savings and loans pay interest on deposits from 5.25% to 7.75%, depending on the term of the deposit. This money on deposit is then loaned out at 8.5% to 10.5%. The gross profit is the difference in these rates. Usually, a bank or savings and loan can break even with a 0.5% differential; anything over the 0.5% spread is profit.

Also operating in the money market is the "secondary money market." Two of its members are the Federal National

Mortgage Association, nicknamed "Fanny Mae", and the Government National Mortgage Association, known as "Ginny Mae". These two organizations act to add liquidity to the financial industry. This is accomplished by buying seasoned mortgages at discounted rates from lending institutions. For example, a bank or savings and loan which lacks liquidity (ample cash) and wishes to make more loans, can sell an existing mortgage to the secondary market, and then take the proceeds and loan them out again. Both associations can buy an existing 9% mortgage for about 8.5% and earn the half of a percent spread as a profit. The loan purchased must be a seasoned, which means prompt payments have been made by the borrower for an extended period of time, thereby representing a good payment record. Most of the time a package of various loans is put together and sold to the secondary market, rather than one individual loan.

TYPES OF LOANS

Although various forms of loans are available, I intend to only list the basic types you will be involved with.

Blanket Mortgages are loans which cover more than one property. This type of loan is required when more financing is required then can be obtained from an individual property. Lenders can then spread their risk over more than one property, which justifies heavier financing. Blanket mortgages are also applicable when several properties are bought, or in subdividing land for new construction.

First Mortgages and Deeds of Trust are instruments for loans based on real property. Should the borrower default on the loan, mortgages and trust deeds allow the lender to foreclose on the property to redeem his money. These forms of loans offer lower interest rates due to the relatively low risk for the lender. The term "first" mortgage designates the loan which is first recorded against a particular property. A second mortgage or second trust deed is lower in priority than a first mortgage or trust deed. Trust deeds are basically the same as mortgages; only trust deeds allow a lender more control in speeding the process of foreclosure, when it is necessary to do so.

Land Contracts or Contracts of Sale are becoming very popular among investors who wish to consumate a sale without involving a lending institution. The purpose of this type of transaction is to offset the purchaser's lack of an adequate down payment or credit. It's strictly a contract between buyer and seller; where the seller retains title until the contract is paid in full, while the buyer retains possession of the property. Interest paid to the seller is usually lower than existing market rates, and the seller can legally get repossession should the buyer default on the land contract.

Chattel Loans are mortgages secured through the collateral of personal property, not real property (real estate). Personal property, such as an automobile, furniture, or business equipment, is the security for the loan. Chattel loans are made for a short term and the interest rates can be twice the rate of conventional mortgages and trust deeds.

Commercial Loans are the best source of short term money and usually require a simple signature; only if your credit and financial statement are worthy enough. These loans are best used for seasonal expenses and purchases, like taxes and equipment on sale. Commercial loan interest rates are usually slightly higher than conventional mortgage rates.

Personal Loans, unlike commercial loans, are made for personal use rather than for business, and are usually paid back in installments. Credit unions and finance companies use this type of loan as interest rates are charged on the unpaid balance at a rate of 12 to 18%.

Home Improvement Loans are easy to obtain and can be used for remodeling, repairs, and additions. Terms can vary up to five years and regular monthly payments are standard. Various forms of this type of loan are available, including funds insured by FHA, known as FHA Title I Home Improvement Loans. Interest rates are slightly higher than home mortgage rates, but still an excellent source of financing.

Personal Loans from relatives are a proven source for the newly wed couple purchasing their honeymoon nest; or even for further investment into income property. Often, relatives will offer low interest rate loans wherein only interest has to be paid over an extended period; then the principal can be paid once the borrower is better established financially.

Existing FHA and VA loans. These are loans that are currently on the books of banks and savings and loans, wherein the current owner of a property is still paying off on the loan. The advantage is that these loans are completely assumable to anyone without any credit qualification whatsoever. These government backed loans continue to be a sure method of financing as they remain intact for the full term of the original loan. You can purchase an existing loan; then, turn around and sell that property to an unqualified buyer where he assumes the same existing loan.

STRUCTURING SECONDARY FINANCING

During the course of many real estate transactions, the necessity of secondary financing enters in to assist in consumating the transaction. Often, conventional financing will not be sufficient, along with down payment, to accomodate the 100% purchase price. For example, the local savings and loan will only lend 80% of sales price, the buyer will only put up a 10% down payment, therefore, a balance of 10% additional financing would be required. This 10% would be handled by the seller in the form of a second mortgage or second trust deed.

Occassionally, more than two loans can be involved with a particular property. There is no greater risk to the owner of the property with two or more loans than with one, providing the terms allow the property to earn enough income to make the payments. Please note that most second mortgages are of shorter duration than the first loan, and care should be taken when balloon payments are attached to loans when planning the property's investment future. Balloon payments result when the balance of the loan is not paid off during its specified term, leaving a balance owing to be paid in full at the end of the term.

While each income producing property is a business in its own right, income left to spend, expenses, and debt service, are very important in a sale. Therefore, you must negotiate for ideal secondary financing in order to attain the highest return on your investment.

Normally, secondary financing involves a term of three to five years, and carries an interest rate higher than a first mortgage. Monthly payments typically are one percent of the total amount financed, ie, a secondary loan for $10,000 will equal monthly payments of $100. In order to attain more spendable income for the owner, secondary financing can be structured to the buyer's advantage by reducing the monthly payment to $75 from $100 per month, and also increasing the term of the payments beyond five years.

In today's real estate market, one fact stands out like a searchlight in the darkest hour of night...investors buy financing, and property prices react accordingly. Terms of financing usually dictate the saleability of any income producing property. As interest rates on income producing property rise, market prices fall; because higher interest rates mean higher monthly payments to pay off the loan, which results in less spendable income. Income property's value is directly related to income. Therefore, due to the same reasons of income, when interest rates decline, market values of income property will increase.

WAYS TO BUY

The price you pay isn't nearly as important as the financial terms you arrange when buying. Since you will want to expand as rapidly as possible, you will want to utilize leverage to your greatest advantage. In order to use leverage properly, it will be necessary to buy using as small a down payment as possible. The following "Ways to Buy" are listed in order of priority alowing the maximum amount of leverage.

Buy VA. This is probably the most advantageous way to buy. The Veterans Administration guarantees a qualified veteran buyer against default on the loan. In other words, if the lender on a VA purchase has to foreclose on the loan because the veteran did not make payments, the VA guarantees the lender against any loss to the lender. At the time of this writing the VA guaranteed a maximum loan of $70,000 on a single family residence, or up to four units, and has to be owner occupied. This type of purchase requires no down payment with only minor closing costs charged to the buyer. Another advantage of buying VA is that when it comes time for the owner to sell, the VA loan is completely assumable to any new buyer without qualifying for a loan (No credit history is required).

Buy Land Contract. (Also known as a contract of sale). This method is popular mainly in the Midwest whereby the seller retains title to the property and the buyer makes payment to the seller. There is no financial intermediary involved; the seller is also the lender. Should the buyer default on his obligation, the property reverts back to the seller. This type of purchase is most advantageous when a condition of "tight money" exists and high interest rates are prevalent. Often you can arrange for an interest rate with the seller which is substantially lower than market rates, plus the seller may be willing to accept a small down payment. Seller's who aren't in need of ready cash for their equities are best suited for a land contract. Check with local real estate laws regarding the land contract.

Buy FHA. This type of purchase enables the Federal Housing Administration to insure lenders of first mortgages on homes against default. Down payment usually varies from 3 to 10%. (FHA is continually changing requirements; see your local realtor for current down payment requirements). This type of loan is also completely assumable as is the VA during the full term of the loan.

VA and FHA Resales. These are properties upon which the VA and FHA have foreclosed. After foreclosure, contractors are sent in to recondition the homes and make them saleable. They are then turned over to select brokers for resale. They are sold in a "as is" condition and usually for less then 10% down with a minimum of closing costs. The loans are also assumable without qualifying for both VA and FHA resales.

Conventional Financing. This is a standard way of financing

whereas the lender will make a maximum loan of 80% on the property and the buyer puts 20% down. This is the least desirable method of financing mainly because of the high down payment needed to acquire the property. Other disadvantages are higher closing costs and pre-payment penalties if the loan is paid off prematurely.

Paying All Cash. Although this method of purchase ties up a lot of cash, it can be advantageous if you can buy substantially below market price. Usually one can purchase below market for all cash from a distressed seller who is in a hurry to make a deal. Then, if you can buy for 20% below market, turn around and get a loan of 80% of market value, you have literally bought a property with no money of your own and picked up 20% equity in the meantime. You can then use the proceeds of the loan to purchase other properties.

Even under not so advantageous offerings, often you can finance your purchases with conventional loans by adding the extra dimension of secondary financing. Since the lender will only loan a maximum of 80%, you have to come up with the difference, either in cash, or by the seller carrying back a second loan.

Carrying back a second loan is a situation wherein the seller agrees to accomodate the buyer with a partial loan on the property he is selling. The situation occurs when the buyer desires to purchase a property with a less than standard down payment (20%) combined with a first loan from a financial institution which doesn't add up to 100% of the full purchase price. An example is wherein a buyer wishes to purchase a home for 100,000. The financial institution involved will make only a maximum loan of 80% ($80,000). The buyer wishes only to put 10% down ($10,000). In order to make up the remaining $10,000 difference in the purchase price, the seller would have to agree to carry back a second loan. This second loan of $10,000 would be paid by the buyer directly to the seller, principal plus interest, on a monthly basis for a negotiated period of time.

These secondary loans usually have a term of three to ten years, depending on the financial needs of the seller. The interest rate often is slightly less than the long term rate charged by the lending institution involved on the first mortgage.

PROPERTY SELECTION

At this point it is my intention to show you how to select your first property. You have available various options of what type of property to invest in: lower income, apartments, and medium and upper income homes. I will discuss the advantages and disadvantages of them all. Once you find the particular type that suits your needs and financial capabilities, you can begin your investment campaign. Keep in mind that in order to attain financial independence, a step-by-step plan of buying, borrowing, selling, and reinvesting beyond your first property will be required. To make the most of your investments and accomplish financial independence, these cardinal principles must be followed:

1. Buy only property that needs improvement.
2. Make only improvements that increase value.
3. Borrow the maximum that can be safely repaid, for the longest period of time, with the smallest monthly payment.
4. Sell at a profit and continue to reinvest.

How you can best execute these principles will be discussed as we progress.

The types of property that are available to you have certain characteristics you should be aware of before you decide which is best for you. Lower income property has the advantage of being easy to buy. VA and FHA financing is readily available and you can assume the loans of these properties for a low, or almost nothing down in some cases. The disadvantages are that they don't sell as quickly as prime property, are harder to manage, and rent is harder to collect due to unemployment, etc. Since this type of property is not as desirable as prime property, obviously it is harder to sell. Most sellers are willing to carry large amounts of secondary financing just to liquidate. You will have to consider this if you buy low income property, because at some point you will be a seller yourself under similar circumstances. Another disadvantage is that it doesn't appreciate as much as prime property; however lower income property usually offers a higher net income mainly due to the higher risk involved.

With prime property, the disadvantage is that it requires more of a down payment to purchase and it usually doesn't allow as much of a net cash flow. However, it has the advantage of appreciating more than low income property, is easier to rent, has a lower vacancy rate and rent loss factor, and is easier to sell. Keep these facts in mind while deciding on what type of property to involve yourself with. My first investments were of the lower income type, and they were always extremely profitable. I had my problems, and these properties were on the market for a long time when I decided to sell, but I always made a handsome profit when the right buyer finally came around, which they eventually do.

The reason for buying only property that needs improvement is that you want to produce a capital gain to expedite expansion of your holdings. You do this by making improvements that cost less than new construction, so that the cost of the older building plus the cost of renovation total less than the cost of a comparable new building.

The property you select should be of sound design and construction where you can make visible tranformations at minimum cost. Improvements such as painting, replacing old fixtures, landscaping, and renovating architectural features, will increase the value substantially.

Your investment should pay a fair return, at least sufficient for covering debt payments and expenses, and it should promise sustained and possibly increased rents. If you invest in lower income property, plan so your net income is no less than 9% of your total investment after debt service and expenses. If you invest in prime property, it may be necessary to sustain a negative cash flow (spending money out of your own pocket) while owning the property until you can raise rents or sell for a profit. In either case, after the property is sold, and you add a substantial capital gain to overall income derived, your net income received will be obviously much higher than the income received while operating the property.

BUYING TIPS

Flexibility is one of the best tools you can carry with you when it finally comes time to negotiate a real estate purchase. More often than not, both buyers and sellers are confronted with a situation in which each party is a few hundred dollars away from agreeing on a price. Sometimes that few hundred dollars, or an antique lamp that the seller won't part with and the buyer must have, keeps the deal from going through. Don't let this happen to you. Be flexible!

While you're out inspecting prospective investments, here are a few methods used by successful investors to determine age, remaining useful life, and type of construction.

Without relying on sellers and real estate brokers, you can determine the accurate age of a building. Simply remove the water closet cover (toilet) located in the bathroom, turn it upside down and read the date engraved inside. This imprint reveals the date of manufacture and is approximately three months prior to the date of construction of the building. Be careful of a bathroom that may have been added on to the house at a later date. Another way to determine age is to locate the electric or gas meter on the building. Normally you will find a date inscribed on it which denotes date of installation of that meter which will coincide with the date that building was built.

When appraising older exterior paint, see if it is aging naturally by powdering or chalking, or if it is blistering, peeling, or flaking. The latter is evidence of condensation between the walls, which causes rapid paint decay.

Leaky roofs can be detected on a dry day by noticing dark stains on the ceiling in the interior of the building.

Curled and broken shingles with shingle debris in and about the gutter and downspout mean the roof is eroding, and a new roof, not patching, will be needed. Split seams on the surface or spots barren of mineral surfacing, normally mean at least patching will be necessary.

Some tip offs of cheap construction are a wall heater without a thermostat, a tiny stall shower without a tub, a deep sink installed in the kitchen to be used for washing clothes and as a kitchen sink.

Should you decide to buy real estate that is listed with a broker, keep in mind that the seller pays the commission, not the buyer. Real estate commissions are usually 6% for most residential properties and 10% on vacant land. Commissions for larger, improved properties can be negotiated downwards, sometimes to less than 5%.

Knowing why the owner is selling can be very helpful at times. The following are the most common reasons:

* Personal reasons, such as illness or death in the family or a divorce.
* Instability of an owner's economic condition.
* An owner wishing relief from managment because of age, desire to travel, etc.
* Change in the neighborhood, especially if the property is owner occupied.
* Deferred maintenance, to the extent where deterioration has occured causing change in tenancy, vacancy, and reduction of the income stream.

Unlike single family homes, multi-unit income property represents a more rational sale, whereas the transfer of title is made for solid business reasons, rather than emotional whims. Every individual property has its own character about it, its own opportunity and style. The task of the alert investor is to match those properties with his own personality and desire, to prosper together to eventual financial independence.

CASHFLOW

Cash flow comes in two forms, positive and negative. Defined, it is the amount of actual cash an investor will receive after operating expenses and debt service are deducted from gross income. Usually, the amount of cash flow you receive from a property will depend on the amount of down payment invested. The more of a down payment, the more positive cash flow.

Positive cash flow can also be available when purchasing lower income property in most cases. However, with prime residential property, often a 10 or 20% down payment will result in a negative cash flow. Which means that gross income of the property will not cover debt service and expenses requiring an "out-of-pocket expense" by the owner. This "out-of-pocket expense" is negative cash flow. An example is if you purchase a three bedroom home for rental purposes and total expense and debt service are $500 per month. You rent to a family for $450 per month, a comparable rent for the area. In order to meet your obligations, you require $50 out of pocket.

Obviously, positive cash flow is better than negative cash flow. But negative cash flow is really not that important because in the prime areas where negative flow is prevalent, homes often appreciate 10 to 20% a year or so which means you can raise rent or sell at a profit. Then, you'll only experience a negative cash flow situation for a year; when you rerent for a higher price you can experience a positive cash flow.

PROCESS OF APPRAISAL

Professional real estate appraisers use three primary methods to determine the value of property; reproduction cost, capitalization or income approach, and market data, sometimes known as the comparable sales approach. We will concentrate on the latter two since the professionals use these most often.

The comparable sales approach is used only in determining the value of single family homes. When determining the value of multi-unit income property, we will use both methods of comparable sales and the income approach.

Please note that the price you pay for a property isn't really that important as long as the price does not deviate too much from the approximate market value. I'm not trying to say go out and pay any arbitrary price for a property. What is more important than the price is the location of the property, its condition, and the financial terms.

It's been said that the three most important things to consider when buying real estate are location, location, and location. A home in a prosperous upper income neighborhood can be worth four times that of a similar home adversely located. In the same community, a home facing a railroad track is worth substantially less than a home fronting a lovely park. Busy streets are often desirable for a retail store, but for a residence, they are consider a noisy hazard. Location is the most potent yardstick for evaluating real estate...but a difficult question to answer is how much is the location worth? The best answer to that is compare two homes that are alike, but in different locations. Compare, and the price differential will be the value of location.

Location is important geographically, like best weather locale in the overall community, or that shopping is nearby. It also means that a subdivision is free from immediate encroachment of adverse commercial developments. But it also means that all identical homes in a subdivision, some may be better located than others. Even in a depressed neighborhood, some homes have a better location than others.

A well-located neighborhood is the number one desire for both tenants looking to rent and buyers planning on purchasing. Good location for residential homes is often associated with good transportation, nearby shopping, quality school districts, and freedom from adverse zoning conditions, such as commercial manufacturing, railroads, etc.

Characterisitcs that make for a bad neighborhood are substandard buildings, overcrowded apartments, overcrowding of the land with buildings leaving no room for grass and trees, and poorly planned land usage where truck terminals are adjacent to churches. Undesirable neighborhoods, tenements and slums are all spawned by the above painful conditions.

The condition of the property is important in your selection because you will want to avoid heavy cash outlays for improvements that won't add value. If a property merely requires cosmetic fix-up, like paint and landscaping, then you may have a bargain at hand. However, major structural damage, such as termite damage, unseen roof decay, or a flimsy foundation can lead to expenditures that may outweigh their value of improvement.

COMPARABLE SALES APPROACH

Determining value by comparable sales approach is basically comparing the subject property, the one you're appraising, with property of a similar nature in the same neighborhood. In a housing tract where all the homes are identical, it is rather simple to take sales within the past six months and compare them with your subject property. If there aren't any differences, like square footage or ameninites like pool, or additional fences, sprinklers, and rooms, then you can assume that if a similar home to yours sold for $62,000 2-weeks ago, your home should be valued about the same. See your local realtor or title company for comparable sales information.

The true art of appraising gets a little more sophisticated when your subject property varies from the 2 or 3 comparables being used. Now you have to add or subtract those added amenities which make the difference between the subject property and the comparables.

Take for an example a subject property which has 1800 square feet of living area, a 2-car garage, is a 3-bedroom, 2-bath located on a standard 60' by 150' lot. You have found two homes in the area that are similar, except they're both 2,000 square feet in size and have 4-bedrooms. Both of the comparable homes sold 30 days ago for $70,000. Now you have to determine what that extra 200 square feet is worth to determine the value of your subject property. By examining overall sales in your neighborhood, you determine that homes are selling for about $35 per square foot of living area. 200x$35 equals $7,000. All else being equal, you determine that your subject property is worth $63,000 because the comparables have 200 more square feet at $35/foot.

The important thing to remember is to add and subtract all items of value concerning both the subject property and the comparables so that you end up equalizing the comparisons to the subject. Sometimes it may be difficult to determine the value of a view or of location, but try to be as rational and honest as you can to be accurate.

VALUATION BY INCOME APPROACH

Income approach, often referred to the "capitalization approach" deals with the present and future value of income from the property. Return *on* investment is considered as well as return *of* the investment as the buildings and equipment depreciate physically. To determine market value using the income approach we must deduct taxes, insurance, all costs of maintenance and net operating income is then divided by a suitable "capitalization rate", and the result is a capitalized market value.

Capitalization rate is a rate of return an investor expects on his investment. It takes into consideration risk of the investment and quality of the income. While appraising income property, one must select a capitalization rate that is applicable. For example, a prime income building located in the best part of town could have a cap. rate of 8%, while a lower income building near adverse zoning could have a cap rate of 10 to 11%. The reason for the higher cap rate is because an investor would expect a higher rate of return because of the quality of the income and the higher risk involved.

Capitalization rates are arbitrary figures determined by an investor as to what rate of return he requires to make an investment compared to other investments.

INCOME PROPERTY ANALYSIS

Scheduled Gross Annual Income		$ 40,000
Less: Vacancies	2,000	
Taxes	4,800	
Insurance	1,000	
Utilities	1,200	
Repairs and Maint.	2,200	
License & Advertising	300	
Payroll	0	
Management	2,400	
Supplies	500	
Services	0	
Furn. & Equip. Reserves	1,600	
Total Vacancy & Expenses		$ 16,000
Net Operating Income		$ 24,000

Taking the above Net Operating Income and dividing it by an applicable capitalization rate will give you a capitalized value. Note that the higher the rate of capitalization, the lower the value, and the lower the rate of capitalization, the higher the value derived.

Example of Captilization:

Net operating Income $24,000 - cap rate (10%) = value of $240,000

Net operating Income $24,000 - cap rate (11%) = value of $218,182

Continuing the Income Property Analysis to give you an entire view of the total property's income statement.

Net Operating Income	$24,000
Less: Loan Payments (P & I) -9,600	
Gross Spendable Income	$14,400
Plus: Principal Payment +600	
Gross Equity Income	$15,000
Less: Depreciation -12,000	
Real Estate Taxable Income	$ 3,000

The following items define more thoroughly the items listed on the Income Property Analysis.

Scheduled Gross Annual Income; the total yearly rent at 100% occupancy.

Less Vacancy; established by the use of existing vacancy ratio for similar buildings in the neighborhood. A good average figure to use is 5% if you do not have an accurate figure. 5% is the national average.

Taxes; actual taxes for the current year.

Insurance; The total annual premium for all forms of insurance associated with the building. If the insurance is part of blanket coverage for several buildings, you must adjust accordingly.

Utilities; a figure for a full year's operation of gas, water, and electricity.

Repairs and Maintenance; 5% of gross scheduled income is a normal estimate.

License & Advertising; Use actual figures of advertising and license fee cost for the entire year.

Payroll; includes payroll taxes and unemployment compensation. This item is used for additional employees, such as a gardener, janitor, or anyone classified as an employee, except the resident manager.

Management; Surveys indicate that a reasonable salary to pay a resident manager is a range of $5 to $17 a month per apartment in the building. Professional management companies are paid a percentage of actual rents collected in addition to the resident manager's salary. Put all management costs on this item.

Supplies; Rent forms, cleaning supplies, and all small items not covered elsewhere are under this category.

Services; Gardening and pool service, etc. are under this category.

Furniture & Equipment Reserves; A contingency fund to be used in reserve for replacing carpeting, drapes, and furniture, and any mechanical equipment which will later need replacing.

Total Vacancy & Expenses; A sum of all the above vacancy and expense items.

Net Operating Income; The result of deducting total vacancy and expenses from scheduled gross income. This figure represents what the property would earn if purchased for cash, free and clear of all debt...NOI is also used to capitalize the value of income, dividing an applicable cap rate into NOI denotes a capitalized value of the subject property.

The remainder of items are self-explanatory and are adjusted income levels to financing and depreciation.

HOW TO BUY

Real estate invariably sells substantially below the asking price; however, property that is relatively fresh on the market tends to sell closer to the asking price. The reason for this is that the seller isn't quite as anxious during the early stages his property is on the open market. Once a property has been on the market for a few months, especially without any offers to purchase, a seller will sometimes accept offers up to twenty-per-cent below his original asking price, although he would refuse such an offer the first week his property was on the market.

Assuming that the seller's price is too high to begin with, subtracting twenty-per-cent from the asking price is not a sure gauge to value, but the resulting figure can be a starting guide after considering other factors. Before establishing a firm figure to offer the seller, consider the lowest possible price the seller might accept; then compute the top price you would offer.

Now you have established upper and lower parameters that you can work within, avoiding any emotional attachment to the property or sales pressure from any third parties. Note any defects in the property and keep them in mind. They will be used to assist you with the initial offer. These defects can be used to pull down the seller's high expectations when negotiations begin to take place.

MAKING THE OFFER

Just for starters...don't assume anything. Keep everything in writing. Most states do not enforce verbal agreements or offers because they're usually only worth the thin air they're spoken on.

Normally, the formal offer in writing includes a good faith deposit as consideration. The amount of deposit will vary from $500 to $2,000, or more depending on the value of the subject property. It is very important that the ingredients of the offer are accurate and clear because in most states the offer is binding when the seller accepts all terms of the contract. However, the offer can be retracted anytime prior to acceptance by the seller.

Your offer should specify a time period by which it is to be accepted. This will eliminate the seller using your offer for leverage against other interested buyers and their offers. Normally three to ten days is customary. Also included in the offer is the date, specified personal property you wish in the deal, down payment, all financial arrangements, and all conditions of the sale.

Financing, and all proposed terms must be clearly spelled out, also, a contingency included stating that the sale is "subject to securing adequate financing." Otherwise, if proper financing cannot be secured, the buyer would forfeit his deposit to the seller.

In the case of an offer for a multi-unit building, conditions of the sale should include a provision for final inspection of all the tenant occupied units. Like "subject to inspection and approval of buyer of each individual unit of the building". This provision will save time should your offer not be accepted; then you haven't wasted time inspecting individual units and upsetting tenants.

Sometimes buyers tend to experience emotions of "cold feet" or that overused terms of "buyers remorse", which is basically caused by a lack of confidence in one's own ability. These queezy feelings can be overcome when the astute investor does all his homework properly and realizes that acceptance of his offer will result in magnificent rewards expected of the subject property he attempts to own.

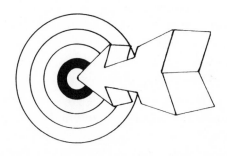

PROPERTY MANAGEMENT

Management of your estate can take the form of a breath-taking challenge...or a daily burdensome chore. It all depends on how conscientious you are in following through with what you are about to learn. Should most of your investment acquisitions be in the form of single family residences, then management can be quite simple, especially if you rent solely to good paying tenants. Simply have your tenants mail in rent from the houses you own. If you decide to get involved with multi-unit apartment buildings, then the ideal position for you to be in is simply over-seeing all your resident managers who are responsible for the management of each individual building.

Ideally, you will have competent resident managers throughout your entire estate which will allow you to make only major decisions and policies for your clientele and managers to follow. Then, you can devote your time to acquiring more property, or just about anything you wish to.

The secret to successful management is turning over as much responsibility as you can to ones manager. Where you only make once a month visits to the property for inspection or rent collection.

Whether you own just one rental house or a vast number of apartment units, you still need to oversee the operation of your property to get the most out of it. You can have a professional property management firm handle your properties. However, this will cost you 5 to 10% of the gross collected rents, depending on the character of your property. I recommend hiring a management firm only when you plan to be absent from the area over an extended period, or, when you purchase extremely large properties. Otherwise, you as an owner can out produce a sometimes inefficient management firm. Once you get the system (which I plan to teach you,) down to a science, it is much better to put that 5 to 10% back into your own pocket.

Before I get into the actual management of your property, it would be wise to decide on certain policies you should pursue. The best way I know to accomplish this is to explain the benefits and disadvantages of each particular situation, then let you decide for yourself which policy will suit your needs best.

FURNISHED Vs. NON-FURNISHED UNITS

Throughout the United States there has been a trend towards unfurnished units. Less turnover among your tenants is the biggest advantage here because it requires more effort by the tenant to move furniture in and out. If you, the owner, supply the furniture, you have that initial expense plus the responsibility of maintaining it.

On the other hand, if you own units which have single or studio type apartments, it may be difficult to rent these units without furniture. Single and studio type apartments thrive on active, transient tenants. They usually require furnishings before they move in.

APPLIANCES

Appliances, such as stoves, refrigerators, and air conditioners, are extremely expensive to maintain. For lower income units, I have found it advantageous *not* to supply any of these items whatsoever. This is somewhat typical, as you will find most lower income families are accustomed to supplying their own stove and refrigerator. Better quality apartments usually require more appliances. If this is the case in your units, be sure it is reflected in your rental rate and the amount of deposit you require. In the case of renting a single family home, refrigerator and stove are often bought with the home, or the stove is built in and can't be removed when the home is sold. Then, rent the home with the appliances included, rather than store them elsewhere.

UTILITIES AND TRASH

In most apartment buildings, especially newer models, separate meters to measure gas and electricity consumption are provided for each apartment; and the respective companies bill the individual tenants. The owner of the building is responsible for paying the water bill. When separate meters are not available, the owner must add the cost of gas and electric to the rent and hope that the tenants are efficient in their use of energy. If you plan to own a building which lacks separate meters for each unit, consider making the change to separate meters. You'll be better off in the long run.

When renting out a single family home, simply have the tenants sign up for all the utilities in their own name.

What about providing laundry machines? If so, should you buy your own equipment or lease? In most cases, especially with eight units or less, it may be wiser not to have machines at all because they will not be used enough to pay for the extra utility expense.

My personal experience with laundry machines has been very profitable. I have two washers and two dryers in a 19-unit family building. The gross monthly receipts from the coin operated machines are between $150 and $200 per month. Of this, the leasing company keeps 60% and sends me a check for the remaining 40%, or $60 to $80 monthly. The leasing company is responsible for maintaining the equipment and the collection of the coins; the owner is responsible for paying for the utilities.

Usually, with eight units or more, washers and dryers will pay for themselves within one or two years. Of course, you must maintain the equipment and be responsible for any acts of vandalism or theft.

If you decide to lease laundry equipment, be sure to have your resident manager oversee the removal of coins from the machines when the collection man makes his rounds. This will eliminate the temptation of his "pocketing" some of your income. Of course, if the manager and the leasing rep are in cahoots, there is little you can do.

CARPETING

Wall-to-wall carpeting will undoubtedly add warmth and value to your units. However, before you go overboard, you must consider the expense compared to the return in rental income. Instead of wall-to-wall coverage, you can keep carpeting to a minimum by using linoleum in the entrance and hallways, and even dining areas. Linoleum will last longer than carpet and will save you plenty of money.

When you do purchase carpeting, use a gold tweed shag of good quality. Gold tweed matches almost any furnishings and doesn't show stains as readily as other colors. Shag carpeting has the advantage over other types of being easier to patch. Later, when you have acquired many properties, if you stick with one standard type and color of carpet, you will be able to buy in large quantities, which will offer substantial savings.

The carpeting industry is very competitive with plenty of suppliers. Therefore, it is best to shop around and get your best price. Many installers moonlight and will install carpet for less than a large distributor.

TENANT PROFILE

Families with children like to live in a building with other families who have children. Likewise, adults without children prefer to live where only adults reside. Senior citizens enjoy living with other older folks, and singles prefer living with other (young) singles. Therefore, you must determine what your tenant profile will be in your multi-unit buildings. (If you're renting a single family residence, a tenant profile is not required.) Utilizing a tenant profile helps to eliminate costly turnover of tenants. You can reduce turnover by keeping the same type of clientele in each of your buildings. Your tenants will then be more likely to develop friendships with their neighbors, which will make them less likely to move.

On the other hand, if you decide on a family building and continue to allow singles to move in, you'll find that most of your time is spent putting up vacancy signs, which is most unprofitable.

Now that we have highlighted some of the policies you will be involved with, it's time to get into the operation of your property. Now that you have acquired your property, we'll assume you need a tenant to occupy your newly acquired prized possession.

ADVERTISING

While your vacant apartment may be the greatest rental in the city, if the public doesn't know it is available, it will remain vacant indefinitely. On the other hand, if you fill the unit with an undesirable, non-paying deadbeat, you'll wish it had remained vacant. There are enough qualified prospects who will treat your property with tender loving care (without attempting financial suicide by renting to deadbeats). The fastest way to bankruptcy, or at least to a heavy-weight migraine headache is to continually rent to non-paying deadbeats.

Alerting prospects to your available unit is best accomplished by using vacancy signs and classified advertising in your local newspaper. Vacancy signs must be precise and to the point, qualifying the prospective tenant to a certain degree. For example, "Vacancy 1-Bedroom, Adults Only", or "Vacancy, 2-Bedroom, Kids OK". By stating certain important facts about the unit, you will eliminate unqualifed prospects who are looking for something other than what you have to offer.

Vacancy signs should be legible and large enough so they can be seen easily from a passing car. Signs must also be placed where they get maximum exposure, either on the side of your building, or on the lawn near the busiest street.

Classified advertising should also be precise in order to eliminate unnecessary calls from unqualified prospects. The four basic principles of good advertising are "A I D A" (Attention, Interest, Desire, and Action). Attention....means the headline of your ad should attract specific prospects to your property. Interest...is expansion of the headline, offering a benefit to your prospect which makes him read the balance of your ad.

Desire...makes the prospect want what you have to offer by using good descriptive copy. Action...means making the prospect respond to your offer.

ATTENTION...could be a heading like "Newly Decorated" or "Large 2-Bedroom". The purpose of the attention heading is to get the reader to distinguish your ad from all the other ads in the column.

INTEREST...must offer a benefit like "New Dishwasher, Newly Carpeted" or "Great Ocean View". This will entice the reader to finish reading the remainder of your offer.

DESIRE...will describe precisely what you have to offer. Like "2-Bedroom, kids OK, $225", or "1-Bedroom., adults only, pool, $195".

ACTION...can be simply a phone number for the reader to call.

Classified advertising is "classified" under specific headings and there is no need to duplicate information that is already available. In other words, it isn't necessary to state that your unit is furnished when you are advertising in the furnished apartment column; or stating that you are downtown when you are under a column denoting specific areas of the city.

RENTING TO THE PROSPECT

Now that you have properly located your vacancy signs and your classified advertising is running in the local newspaper, it is time to market your unit to potential tenants. In most cases, your prospect will have telephoned you from your ad or from the phone number on your vacancy sign. At this point your prospect will require the exact address and further details about the available unit. Your salesmanship begins here as you can reply enthusiastically about all features and benefits of your unit.

Make an appointment to show the unit after further qualifying the prospect, and, of course, if the potential tenant is still interested. If it is a husband and wife, be sure to have them see the unit together to avoid separate showings to each at different times.

First appearances can tell you a lot about someone's habits; they can also be very deceiving. When your prospects arrive to see your available unit, examine their appearance and their car. Nine times out of ten, a sleezy, beat-up old junker, means their present home will look similar; and that means if you rent to them, you can bet your bippy that your home will end up looking like their jalopy. On the other hand, don't be overwhelmed by a smooth-talking, well-dressed "cat" in a clean Caddy...he may keep your place in great shape, but if he doesn't pay any rent, you're worse off than having the unit vacant.

If a complete stranger approached you on the street and said, "I need your car. May I have your keys?" you would probably tell him, "No". Yet, in the real estate rental business, there are many owners who will allow a person or family to come in off the street as complete strangers and move into their property without asking them for any information. Time after time, a tenant will acquire possession of an asset worth thousands of dollars simply by showing up at the door and saying, "I need a place to live". Whether or not he decides to pay rent in the future, he has gained the right to use and enjoy your property and the right to privacy.

Should your new tenant not pay rent, removing him from the premises, requires "due process of law". In California, this means unlawful detainer action; in most other states, an eviction suit. These actions, if successful, will bring only a judgement for rent monies, court costs, and moving fees. Cases that go to court undoubtedly require 20-30 days or more. The costs involved, plus additional loss of rent, can get out of hand when a professional deadbeat decides to slither onto your premises.

The best way to avoid the professional deadbeat is to properly check prospective tenant backgrounds. This begins when the prospect completes the rental application.

When your prospect decides he wants to rent, get a minimum deposit of $50 from him to hold the unit and have him complete a rental application. (See a sample of the rental application in "Forms" section). The deposit acts as a commitment from the prospect. Also, if he later changes his mind, you can at least have an opportunity to resell him when he returns to pick up his deposit.

Once you have a deposit and a rental application completed, inform your potential tenant that you will notify him after his references are checked and send him on his way. You can now make some inquiries with current and past landlords, verify employment, etc. Keep in mind that your tenant's total monthly gross income should be at least three and a half times his monthly rent. This is a good rule of thumb; in fact, often bankers allow a 4 to 1 ratio when determining whether a potential home buyer can afford the monthly payments on a loan.

DEPOSITS

Apart from rent, before right of possession is given to the tenant, certain deposits are necessary to insure the successful operation of your properties. A security deposit is a refundable deposit protecting the owner from damage to the premises. A good rule of thumb on month-to-month tenancy is to charge one month's rent for security. This amount can be adjusted upwards, depending on additional furnishings the owner may supply. Prior to moving in, a tenant should be informed that the security deposit cannot be applied to his rent. It will be refunded only after the management is given proper notice of his intent to vacate and the unit is left in good condition.

Another deposit is the non-refundable cleaning fee. This charge generally runs between $50 and $100 depending on the character of the building. Certain states do not allow a cleaning fee to be charged. If this is the case, you may simply rename it "a one-time leasing charge," non-refundable.

A key deposit is also a necessary charge, refundable when the apartment is vacated and all keys returned to the management. $10 is a good nominal key deposit.

Additional deposits must be charged if you decide to allow pets on the premises. I suggest $100-200 for a pet damage deposit, refundable.

Be sure all rent and deposits are collected before the keys are handed over and possession is given to your tenants, *with no exceptions.*

RENTAL AGREEMENTS

Verbal agreements between landlord and tenant aren't really worth a darn; they are unenforceable in a court of law, (with a few exceptions) and you should avoid them at all costs. Everything must be spelled out in writing to avoid potential disputes. You'll never know when it may be necessary to defend yourself in court and if the rental agreement is in writing you'll have a much better chance of winning your case.

The relationship between owner and tenant is called *tenancy.* It is operated and terminated under very specific laws in each state. You will be primarily involved with fixed and periodic tenancy. *Fixed tenancy* is in effect for a specific period of time, such as one year. Fixed tenancy has an exact starting date and a specific duration. It is not renewed or extended without agreement by both parties. Rent payments do not necessarily coincide with the term of tenancy. Thus, if a tenancy is for one year, as in a one year lease, rent is usually paid on a monthly or yearly basis during that year.

Periodic tenancy involves a continous series of terms, as in a month-to-month rental agreement, rather than a single term. Each term is automatically renewed, unless one of the parties gives notice to terminate the tenancy. Occupation of the premises runs for one month, then starts over and runs for another month. Rent is usually paid on a month-to-month basis. If a tenant doesn't vacate after a month, tenancy becomes periodic when the owner acknowledges the fact by accepting rent.

In the case of a month-to-month agreement, tenant or landlord must give 30-days' notice in order to change the terms of tenancy. These changes could include a notice to vacate by either party or the landlord may decide to raise the rent.

In the case of fixed tenancy, as in a one year lease, both parties have agreed to terms over a one year period and both must abide to their agreement. Tenant is responsible for a year of rent at a specific rate, and the landlord cannot change that rental rate, unless it is specified in the agreement. (See samples of month-to-month and lease agreement in "Forms" section.)

Your rental agreements must be signed by the tenant, the tenant's spouse, and by all adults who will occupy the premises. Where two, three or more are sharing a unit, a clause of "tenants are jointly and severally reponsible for payment of rent," is required for your protection.

At the onset of taking over the ownership of a property, be sure all existing tenants are under a written rental agreement. In the case of renting furnished units, make appointments with the tenants and take an inventory of all furniture. Have the tenants sign the inventory and the new rental agreement at the same time.

RENT COLLECTION

Efficiently managing your real estate will invariably depend on your collection policies. Your real estate investment is purely a money-making business, not a downtown mission run on charity. Owners who yield to non-paying deadbeats cannot meet their own operating costs and may soon end up in bankruptcy.

Rents can be collected very efficiently when the resident

manager and tenants are aware of the procedures, and they are followed. An effective collection policy is to have all rent-payable due dates fall during the first seven days of the month, although exceptions can be made.

Appropriate contract forms should be used. A triplicate rent receipt is necessary with copies for the tenant, the resident manager, and the owner. A reminder notice should be issued when rent is three days past due. If your tenant does not reply to the three day notice, the manager must then make a personal visit to collect. And, if no progress is made on the personal visit, a "3-day pay rent or quit the premises notice" must be issued immediately. (3-day pay or quit is used in California. For eviction processing in other states, check local landlord tenant laws.)

If, after three days, the rent has not been paid without specific reason, the manager must attach a three-day reminder to the tenant's door. This act should be noted under the comment column of the delinquency sheet. Two days after the three-day reminder is issued, the manager must follow up, either personnally or by phone. If no money or response is given, eviction proceedings should begin at once.

Instead of a late fee, which we discussed earlier, to stimulate prompt payment of rent, efficient manager's often give a $10 discount if rent is paid by the due date. If you decide to use this method, you can offset the $10 loss merely by charging $10 more when you initially rent the unit. Then, the base rent would be equal to the discounted rate.

Many sophisticated property managers charge a ten-dollar late fee when rent is more than three days past due. This method is very effective; however, some state laws do not allow it. In most cases I have found that if you enforce this method once, tenants are rarely late a second time.

If you employ a resident manager, he should have a list of all current tenants at the beginning of each month. This will serve as a deliquency list, which will include tenant's name, due date, rent amount, and a comment column. This serves as a ready reference for both manager and owner. As each tenant pays, his name is crossed off the list. On occassion, a tenant will tell the manager that the rent will be paid in two days. This remark will be noted on the delinquency list and followed up on by the manager when the two days has elapsed.

When a tenant has established a good payment history, more lenient allowances can be made when unusual circumstances occur, such as, the loss of a job, illness, or death in the family. Whatever the case, definite commitments must be made and recorded on the delinquency sheet, and followed up on by the manager.

Rent payments must be made in the form of a check or money order and *absolutely not in cash*. This will eliminate temptation of theft, or a manager's possible desire to borrow small amounts of money. Only in the case of an emergency, or when someone is extremely late in paying his rent, should cash be accepted.

RAISING RENTS

After you initially acquire legal ownership of a property and you have tenants existing on the premises, it will probably be necessary at some time to raise the rent. Rental increases are handled the same way as changing any other terms of tenancy. In most states the law requires a minimum of a 30-day notice to inform tenants of the new rental rate. I recommend giving a 45-day notice to allow more consideration for your tenants.

When raising rents, you must always be concerned with the fact that a few of your tenants may decide to move, especially if they can find less expensive, comparable housing. Therefore, it is very important that you know what comparable housing in your neighborhood is renting for. If you keep your rental rates equal to, or below comparable units in the area, the majority of your tenants will surely remain. The cost of moving and the hassle of finding a new place are too much to bear just to find similar housing for the same price.

Should you decide to raise the rent of an entire multi-unit building, raise no more than 25% of the building in any one single month. Then, raise the remainder of the units accordingly each month until you have all the units at comparable rates. Raising only a portion of your building monthly will help to avoid having a large number of vacancies at one time.

The best and easiest time to raise rent is after a vacancy occurs. (For a sample of a rent raise letter, see the chapter on forms.)

THE RESIDENT MANAGER

Should your overall strategy of property acquisition entail purely the purchase of single family homes, it won't be necessary to involve yourself with onsight resident managers.

Once a property is acquired and basic improvements and rental increases have been instituted, an apartment owner should have to spend only a few hours a month with any individual property. When a competent resident manager is on the premises, he can relieve the owner of many time-consuming operations and responsibilities. On the other hand, an incompetent manager can create nagging headaches and needless expense.

In order to reach the stage where only a few hours per month are involved with each property, the owner must delegate as much responsibility to his resident manager as he possibly can. Then you, the owner, will be required to make only major decisions and periodic inspection visits, which will enable you to devote your time to policies involving your entire estate.

After the initial acquisition of a multi-unit property, you will have to decide whether to keep the existing manager or find a new one. Usually, thirty days is enough time to determine the capabilities of the existing manager. Should you not be satisfied with the current manager, it is best to begin looking for a replacement immediately. Good managers are plentiful if you need a replacement, as you will soon find out.

Certain ingredients make for an ideal resident management team. A husband and wife are particularly well-suited for apartments, as the husband can work at a full time job and do repairs part time, while the wife is free to manage full time. The following are the chief qualities found in good managers, which are listed in their order of importance:

1. Eagerness and willingness to do the job properly.
2. Ability to accept responsibility.
3. A husband that is handy at minor repairs and maintenance.
4. A wife with a pleasant personality and a willingness to stay at home and to perform routine housekeeping duties.
5. Honesty.
6. Experience.

Please note that "experience" is listed last in priority of qualities. Many times I have found that it takes more time to weed out so-called experienced managers and their inefficiencies than it takes to completely train an inexperienced manager exactly the way you want things done.

Primarily, the manager's reponsibility is to collect rents, show vacant apartments, and keep the grounds clean. If the man is handy, then you will find that it always isn't necessary to call on a skilled, expensive repair man to do common minor repairs.

It is very important that the manager is on the job to show vacancies and keep order. A wife that is active socially outside the home is not a good prospect; the domestic housewife with children tends to be the best stay-at-homer.

What you pay the manager depends primarily on the size of the building. With a twenty-unit building, free rent is a typical agreement. On a smaller four-plex type building, twenty-five to thirty-three percent of rent on a one-bedroom apartment, depending on the rental rate, is normal. Buildings larger than twenty-units usually involve free rent plus cash salaries. Look in the classified section of your local newspaper under the column "Couples Wanted" for competitive rates and salaries in your area.

MANAGER SUPERVISION

Duties of the resident manager must be fully explained at the onset of the owner-employer relationship. Remember, the more responsibility an owner can delegate to the manager, the more time he has to pursue other matters.

Monthly reports filled out by the manager are absolutely necessary for proper accounting and ready reference. These reports include a list of rents collected for the month, with one copy of rent receipts attached, a delinquency list, and a bank deposit (optional). Larger buildings may include other forms reporting vacancies, future available apartments, etc.

A list of rents collected will include apartment numbers, rent-due and rent-paid dates, amount paid, and type of payments made (rent, cleaning fee, key deposit, or security deposit). One copy of the rent receipt is attached to the rent collected sheet, which the owner puts on file. The other two copies of the triplicate rent receipts are kept by the manager and tenant.

The delinquency report is kept by the manager for ready reference. This form will denote apartment numbers, tenant names, amounts due, and a column for commments. At the first of the month the manager will fill out each apartment number, name, and amount due; then, the manager will cross off each tenant as the rent is paid. Comment column is used for noting the date when a delinquent notice was issued, or for when a tenant makes a promise to pay by a certain date. By making note of all communications with tenants, the manager can efficiently follow up on all collection work.

Bank deposit copies or reports are optional, depending on

whether the manager or the owner makes the necessary deposits.

Monthly supervisory visits by the owner are a good practice. Major decisions on recarpeting or on other costly repairs can be made as well as picking up collected rents and making periodic inspections. Immediately after purchasing a new property, you'll spend more time than usual on it; but, as time goes by and you get better organized, your time will be better spent elsewhere.

Besides monthly reports, your manager must handle renting vacant units, rent collection, and care of the grounds. Each time you make your periodic visit, be sure your manager is maintaining your policies in these matters.

BEYOND YOUR FIRST PROPERTY

Attaining the "Power of Financial Independence" is only accomplished through continually buying, improving, selling, and reinvesting in real estate to produce a geometric rate of progression equal to that of pyramiding. Therefore, once you have acquired your first property, you must begin planning for your second one, which will eventually lead you to future acquisitions.

After acquiring your first property and improving it to its maximum value at that particular time, you will have basically four options available to you. 1. You can simply continue to hold and operate the property for further appreciation. 2. You can sell at a profit and reinvest in a second or third property. 3. You can trade for a larger property. 4. Or, you can refinance your existing property and use the funds to by more properties.

Should you decide merely to hold your investment for further appreciation, your ability to pyramid an estate will be severely hampered. True, you will stay ahead of inflation, and you will receive income from your investment, but you won't gain the financial independence you desire if you don't continually reinvest and expand.

Selling at a profit and reinvesting in a larger property is the ideal strategy to use in the early stages of your real estate investment career. Quick turnover profits will add to your confidence and will give you the needed expertise in executing transactions involving larger parcels later on.

Trading your first property for a larger one is an option available to you. However, it might be better exercised at a later date after you've gained more experience at buying and sellng real estate. Trading properties has two primary advantages over selling and reinvesting, that of avoiding capital gains taxes (capital gains are deferred when real estate is traded) incurred at the time of the transaction, and that of having zero time lag on invested capital during the period required to buy a second property after the first property is sold.

Once your initial property is sold at a profit, there will be a period of time required to initiate the purchase of a second property. During this period, the profit plus equity funds you derived from the sale will be relatively inactive, not earning the potential return they could be if invested in another property. On the other hand, if a trade were initiated, no lag time would result and all funds derived from the trade would continue to be invested in real estate.

At times, it may be wise to retain your property and refinance it to buy other properties. This method is most effective during a period following a boom in real estate prices where it appears the real estate market has temporarily flattened out. You may want to hold on during this buyer's market so you can get a better price later on. In the meantime, you can refinance and make some advantageous purchases during a buyer's market.

When considering the above-mentioned options, an interesting thing occurs to the rate of return on equity dollars you have invested in a property. It diminishes drastically while you hold the property. Let me explain what I mean. Equity dollars are the total amount of money, you, the owner, have invested in a property. This includes the initial down payment, money invested on improvements, and any additional value derived from the improvements and appreciation. For an example, take an apartment building I purchased a few years ago. The initial purchase price was $110,000, with a $9,000 down payment, and $3,000 invested in improvements. The first year of ownership my total investment, or equity position was $12,000.

After making all necessary improvements and increasing rent, the fair market value was $135,000 in the second year of ownership. Now, because of the increased value, my equity position equaled my initial investment of $12,000, plus the increase in property value of $25,000 ($135,000-$110,000), which equaled $37,000 in the second year of ownership. Refer to example below.

Example of Diminishing Return on Equity Dollars

First Year of Ownership

$110,000 Initial cost of property
    9,000 down payment
    3,000 cost of improvement
  12,000 total investment, or equity first year
        $5,400 equals first year income

$5,400 divided by $12,000 equity equals 45% return on equity 1st yr.

Second Year of Ownership

$135,000 fair market value, second year
-110,000 initial cost of property
  25,000 gain in value
  12,000 total investment, or initial equity
  37,000 total equity in second year
        $5,400 equals 2nd yr. income

$5,400 divided by $37,000 total equity 2nd yr. equals 14.6% return on equity 2nd yr.

In the above example, note the diminishing return on equity from the first year to the second. (45% down to 14.6%) The reason for the reduction in the rate of return on equity dollars is the additional value of $25,000 derived from improving the property and appreciation. When the additional amount is divided into the constant net income for both years, the result is a reduced return on equity for the second year. If we projected out over a third year, return on equity would diminish even further below that 14.6% return of the second year.

This effect of diminishing returns on equity dollars is important to remember when you are making decisions as to how long to hold a specific property. Often, once a property has reached a certain value during the early years of ownership where you can derive a substantial profit from a sale or exchange, it is wise to do so to attain maximum return on equity.

In fact, the entire formula for your success in acquiring financial independence will be to maximize your return on invested dollars. Continual reselling or refinancing of your equity position will enable you to progress at a geometric rate of expansion, rather then to maintain a stagnant position of diminishing returns on equity dollars.

BUILDING TO FINANCIAL INDEPENDENCE

Determination and motivation, followed by Planning, Saving, Investing and reinvesting will catapult you to your eventual final objective of financial independence. By utilizing the methods discussed you will make things happen. What many have often referred to as "luck" or "fate" has absolutely nothing to do with your success or failure. Your eventual "luck" will be determined by the proper application of the planning you will use effectively in operating your own business.

You will begin, as discussed earlier, by setting preliminary goals in order to reach your final objective. Your first downpayment of 5 or $6,000 to purchase your first home can be a preliminary goal if you haven't saved it already. Now, what do you have to do to save that much? Eliminate from your daily living what you really don't need in order to save a minimum of 10%. Be positive! Don't look at it as a great sacrifice; instead visualize the magificent home that down payment will bring you.

Drive, belief, enthusiasm are all powerful ingredients for success. However, each quality is somewhat worthless unless directed toward a well thought-out plan. Then, the plan must be executed by using proper methods to lead you to your goal.

You have the methods in front of you; all you have to do now is supply the drive, motivation and execute the plans you'll develop from what I've taught you.

Once you've purchased that first parcel of real estate, keep the adrenilin flowing and begin planning your next preliminary objective. Do not be obsessed with waiting for lower interest rates or waiting for a hypothetical crash in the economy, which doomsday preachers keep predicting. This will only delay your final objective. You must continue to think positively, keeping your goals in sight.

The future of real estate has never been brighter. The market will always have its casual ups and downs, high and low interest rate levels. Just don't get caught up in waiting for the exact moment of turn around. Even the experts can only guess, and most of the time they're wrong. It's your job to keep saving, investing, and reinvesting and not to get involved with predicting market swings. Remember, that it's been over fifty years since the last depression. And even then, real estate faired better than any other asset held by investors.

MAKE YOUR DECISIONS NOW

With strong determination and drive, absolutely nothing can stop you from accomplishing what you set out to do. But you've got to make that decision...that of acquiring the Power of Financial Independence. Make that decision now and stick to it. When you apply everything you've learned in my manual and see that it works, don't stop short! Make it work again and again.

Continue to reinvest your profits and don't ever touch your capital. Later you will have so much money you can spend huge sums on those fancy cars and boats without exploiting your working capital. But do it later, not now when saving your initial capital is so important to your final success.

As you continue to progress toward financial independence, you'll find that your time may be better spent working full time at real estate investment. Initially, a full job is necessary to help you procure investment capital. Later on, after many investments and profits are made, you can reevaluate your existing financial condition to determine what is best for your own future.

Your ability to motivate yourself, plus drive and determination while planning and executing these formulas presented to you, will produce for you the most bountiful harvest of profits you can imagine. It is important to remember that the profits derived will not only advance your standard of living, but allow you the freedom you want today and the Power of Financial Independence you deserve.

SAMPLE MANAGEMENT FORMS

RENTAL APPLICATION

Last Name_____ First_____ Initial_____
Spouse Full Name_____
Apt. to be occcupied by _____ Persons
Present address_____ City_____
State_____ Zip____ How long____ mo's____ yr's.
Applicants birth date_____ Drivers Lic_____
Soc Sec#_____ Spouse birth date_____
Drivers Lic_____ Soc Sec#_____
Present landlord_____ Phone_____
Monthly pymt._____ How long____
Previous landlord_____ Phone_____
Employers Name_____ How long_____
Address_____ Position_____ Salary____
Additional Income_____ Source_____
Applicants closest relative_____
Address_____ Phone_____
Bank_____ Checking acct #_____
Credit reference_____ acct#_____
Credit reference_____ acct#_____
Vehicles_____ Lic#_____
Vehicles_____ Lic#_____
Name &Address of referring party_____

Signature of Applicant:_____
Date:_____

MANAGER' MONTHLY INCOME REPORT

Name	Apt#	Rent	Sec	Key	Lease	Rec#	Total
Laundry							
Total							

Month & Year ____   Total monies collected

Vacant Apts. _____   _____

New Move-ins _____   Manager

DELINQUENCY REPORT

Tenant Name	Apt #	Amount	Comments

REMINDERS TO PAY RENT

May we call your attention to the fact that our records show your rent unpaid for the current period.

We would appreciate your prompt payment.

_____
Manager

FIVE-DAY REMINDER TO PAY RENT

We have not received your rent for the period of _____ amounting to $_____ although you were notified in a previous notice.

As we are required to report at once to the owner we are asking for immediate payment.

_____
Manager

NOTICE TO PAY OR QUIT

TO _____

_____

Within three days after service upon you of this
notice, you are hereby required to pay the rent of
the premises hereinafter described, of which you
now hold possession, amounting to the sum of
_____ Dollars, ($ _____)
at the rental rate of _____ Dollars,
($_____)per month, being the rent due and
owing for the month commencing the _____ day of
_____, 19_____, and _____

_____

or you are hereby required to deliver up possession
of the hereinafter described premises, within three
days after service on you of this notice to _____
_____, the duly authorized agent of the owner of
said premises, or the said owner will institute
legal proceedings against you to recover the possession of said premises with all rents due and owing
and any damages caused to said premises. The
undersigned, as Landlord, hereby declares a fore-
feiture of the agreement under which you occupy the
hereinbelow described premises.

The premises herein referred to are situated
in the City of _____, County of _____
_____, State of California and are
designated by apartment number, number and street
as: _____

_____

_____

_____

Dated this _____ day of _____, 19_____.
By: _____ Name and title

30-DAY NOTICE TO TERMINATE TENANCY

TO _____, TENANT IN
POSSESSION: PLEASE TAKE NOTICE that you
are hereby required within 30 days to remove
from and deliver up possession of the premises
now held and occupied by you, being those premises now held and occupied by you, being those
premises situated in the City of _____,
County of _____, State of California,
commonly known as _____.

This notice is intended for the purpose of terminating the Rental Agreement by which you now
hold possession of the above-described premises,
and should you fail to comply, legal proceedings
will be instituted against you to recover possession,
to declare said Rental Agreement forfeited, and to
recover treble rents and damages for the period
of the unlawful detention.

Please be advised that your rent on said premises
is due and payable up to and including the date of
termination of your tenancy under this notice, that
being the _____ day of _____, 19_____.

Dated this _____ Day of _____, 19___.

_____
Owner/Manager

RENT RAISE LETTER TO TENANTS

NOTICE TO CHANGE TERMS OF TENANCY

TO _____Tenant in possession

_____

_____

    You are hereby notified that the terms of tenancy under which you occupy the above-described premises are to be changed.

    Effective _____, 19 ____, your rent will be increased by _____per month, from _____per month to _____ per month, payable in advance.

    Dated this _____ day of _____, 19 _____.

_____

Owner/Manager

LEASE

This is intended to be a legally binding agreement-
Read it carefully.

Dated _____ 19____ .
_____ California

1. _____ Landlord,
and _____ Tenant,
agree as follows: Landlord leases to Tenant and
Tenant hires from Landlord those premises described as: _____

_____
together with the following furniture and fixtures:__

_____
(If list is extensive, attach hereto as exhibit "A".)
2. The term of this lease shall be _____
commencing _____ 19____ and terminating
_____ 19____ .

3. If the tenant remains in the premises after the
lease expires, and the landlord accepts rent, tenancy
is changed to the term for which the rent is paid,
becoming a periodic tenancy of month-to-month.
4. Tenant agrees to pay rent as follows: _____

_____

NOTE: The remainder of the provisions in this
lease can be duplicated from the MONTH-
TO-MONTH RENTAL AGREEMENT beginning with provision 3.

MONTH-TO-MONTH RENTAL AGREEMENT

This is intended to be a legally binding agreement-
Read it carefully.

Dated _____ 19__
_____ California

1. _____ Landlord,
agrees to rent to _____ Tenant, the
premises described as: _____

_____

together with the following furniture and fixtures:

_____

(If list is extensive, attach hereto as exhibit "A".)
2. The rental shall commence on _____
19 ___, and shall continue from month to month unless otherwise stated here: _____

_____

This rental may be terminated at any time by either
party by giving written notice 30 days in advance,
unless a longer or shorter period of advance notice
is specified here: _____.
   Tenant agrees to pay $_____ rent per
month on the _____ day of each month
_____ at _____
3. Tenant agrees to pay upon execution of this agreement, in addition to rent, a nonrefundable leasing
charge of $_____.
4. Tenant agrees to pay all utilities except _____
which shall be paid for by the landlord.
5. Tenant has examined the premises and all furniture and fixtures contained therein, and accepts
the same as being clean and in good order, condition and repair, with the following exceptions:_____

_____

6. The premises are rented for the use only as a residence for ____ adults and ____ children.

No animal or pet except _____ shall be kept on the premises without Landlord's prior written consent.

7. Tenant may not assign, transfer, or sublet to another person without the written consent of the Landlord.

8. Tenant shall not disturb, annoy, endanger or inconvenience other tenants of the building or neighbors, nor use the premises for any immoral or unlawful purposes, nor violate any law or ordinance, nor commit waste or nuisance upon or about the premises.

9. Tenant shall obey the Rules and Regulations for the property attached hereto.

10. Tenant shall keep the premises rented for his exclusive use in good order and condition and pay for any repairs caused by his negligence or misuse or that of his invitees. Landlord shall maintain any other parts of the property and pay for the repairs not caused by tenant's negligence or misuse or that of his invitees.

11. With tenant's permission, which shall not unreasonably be withheld, Landlord or his agent shall be permitted to enter to inspect, to make repairs, and to show the premises to prospective tenants or purchasers. In an emergency, Landlord or his agent may enter the premises without securing prior permission from tenant, but shall give tenant notice of such immediately thereafter.

12. Tenant shall neither paint nor make alterations of the property without Landlord's prior written consent.

13. If tenant abandons or vacates the premises, Landlord may at his option terminate this agreement,

re-enter the premises and remove all property.

14. The prevailing party may recover from the other party his costs and attorney fees of any action brought by the other party.

15. Either party may terminate this agreement in the event of a violatoin of any provision of this agreement by the other party.

_____   Tenant
  Landlord/Manager   Tenant

CARDEX (TENANT RECORD)

82

PROJ. NAME _____

Orig. Move-In Date _____

Lease Dated _____ Exp. _____

Tenant Tel. No. _____

DEPOSIT

RENT

PARK # _____ KEY SIGNATURE _____ # _____

Date Due	Date Paid	Receipt Number	Paid To Noon	Amount Paid	Security Deposit	Cleaning Fee	Key Deposit #	Base Rent	Refrig-erator	Furniture	Parking	Month to Month	Additional Occupancy	Other Fireplace & Dishwasher	Air Conditioner	Utilities		Total Rent	Balance Due

Date Due

BLDG. # _____ APT. _____ TYPE _____ FL. PL. _____ CLR. _____ NAME _____

DEFINITIONS USED IN REAL ESTATE

ABSTRACT OF TITLE: A summary of the conveyances, transfers, and any other data relied on as evidence of title, together with any other elements of record which may impair the title.

ACCELERATION CLAUSE: A clause in a mortgage or deed of trust giving the lender the right to call all monies owed him to be immediately due and payable upon the happening of a certain stated event.

ACCEPTANCE: refers to a legal term denoting acceptance of an offer. A buyer offers to buy and the seller accepts the offer.

ADMINISTRATOR: An individual appointed by the probate court to administer the estate of a deceased person.

AFFIDAVIT: A written statement or declaration sworn to or affirmed before some official who has authority to administer affirmation.

AGREEMENT OF SALE: A written contract between the buyer and seller, where both parties are at full agreement on the terms and conditions of the sale.

ALIENATION: The transfer of property, or other things from one person to another.

AMORITZATION: The liquidation of a financial obligation using regular equal payments on an installment basis.

APPRAISAL: An estimate and opinion of value; a factual conclusion resulting from an analysis of pertinent data.

APPURTENANCE: Something belonging to the land and conveyed with it, such as buildings, fixtures, rights.

ASSESSED VALUE: Value placed upon property by the tax assessor.

ASSESSMENT: The valuation of property for the purpose of levying a tax, or the amount of the tax levied.

ASSESSOR: One appointed to assess property for taxation.

ASSIGNMENT: A transfer or making over to another the whole of any property, real or personal, or of any estate or right therein. To assign - to transfer.

ASSIGNOR: One who owns property assigned. Assignee - one who receives the property being assigned.

ATTACHMENT: Seizure of property by court order, usually done in a pending law suit to make property available in case of judgment.

BALANCE SHEET: A financial statement which shows true condition of a business as of a particular date; Discloses assets, liabilities and net worth.

BALLOON PAYMENT: The final installment paid at the end of the term of a note; used only when preceding installments did not pay off note in full.

BASE AND MERIDIAN: Imaginary lines used by surveyors to find and describe the location of public or private lands.

BENEFICIARY: The lender on the security of a note and deed of trust. One entitled to the benefit of a trust.

BEQUEATH: To give or leave personal property by a will.

BLANKET ENCUMBRANCE: A single mortgage or trust deed which covers more than one piece of real estate.

BLIGHTED AREA: A declining area where property values are effected by destructive economic or natural forces.

BREACH: Violation of an obligation in a contract.

BUILDING LINE: (Also a setback line) A line set by law or deed restricting a certain distance from the street line, in front of which an owner cannot build on his lot.

BUSINESS OPPORTUNITY: The sale or lease of a business and goodwill of an existing business enterprise.

BUYERS MARKET: More sellers than buyers.

CAPITALIZATION: In appraising, determining value by considering net income and percentage of a reasonable return on investment.

CASH FLOW: Gross income less costs of operating expenses and debt service.

CHAIN OF TITLE: A history of conveyances and encumberances affecting the title as far back as records are available.

CHATTEL MORTGAGE: A mortgage on personal property.

COLLATERAL SECURITY: A separate obligation attached to another contract pledging something of value to guarantee performance of the contract.

COMMUNITY PROPERTY: Both real and personal property accumulated after marriage through joint efforts of husband and wife living together.

COMPOUND INTEREST: Interest paid back on the original principal and on interest accrued from time it became due.

CONDEMNATION: A declaration by governing powers that a structure is unfit for use.

CONDITIONAL SALES CONTRACT: A contract for the sale of property where buyer has possession and use, but, the seller retains title until the conditions of the contract have been fulfilled. A land contract.

CONDOMINIUM: A system of individual ownership of units in a multi-family structure, wherein each owner jointly owns the common areas and the land.

CONSIDERATION: Anything of value given to induce entering into a contract.

CONTRACT: An agreement, written or oral, to do or not to do certain things.

CONVEYANCE: The transfer of the title to land from one to another.

CORPORATION: A legal entity having certain powers and duties of a natural person, together with rights and liabilities of both, distinct and apart from those of the persons composing it

COVENANTS: Agreements written into deeds and other instruments stating performance or non-performance of certain acts or noting certain uses or non-uses of the property.

C.P.M.: Certified Property Manager.

CUL DE SAC: A street open at one end only, a dead end street with turn-around included.

DEED: A written instrument which when executed, conveys title of real property.

DEFAULT: Failure to fulfill or discharge an obligation, or to perform any act that has been agreed to in writing.

DEFERRED MAINTENANCE: Normal upkeep of a property which has been postponed.

DOWER: The right which a wife has in here husband's estate at his death.

EASEMENT: Is the right, privilege, or interest which one party has in the land of another created by a grant or agreement for a specific purpose.

ECONOMIC LIFE: The period over which a property will yield a return on the investment.

ECONOMIC RENT: The current market rental rate based on comparable rent paid for similar space.

EMINENT DOMAIN: The right of the government to acquire

private property for public use by condemnation. The owner must be fully compensated.

ENCROACHMENT: Trespass, the building or structure or any improvements partly or wholly on the property of another.

ENCUMBRANCE: Anything which affects or limits the fee simple title to property, such as mortgages, trust deeds, easements or restrictions of any kind. Liens are special encumbrances which make the property security for the debt.

EQUITY: The value which an owner has in real estate over and above the liens against it.

ESCHEAT: The reverting of property to the state in the absence of heirs.

ESCROW: A neutral third party who carrys out the provisions of an agreement between two parties.

EXCLUSIVE AGENCY LISTING: A written instrument giving one agent the right to sell a property, but reserving the right of the owner to sell the property himself without paying a commission to the agent.

EXCLUSIVE RIGHT TO SELL LISTING: A written agreement between agent and owner, where agent has the right to collect a commission if the property is sold by anyone during the terms of agreement.

FIDUCIARY: A person in a position of trust and confidence, as between principal and broker; broker as a fiduciary owes loyalty to the principal which cannot be breached under rules of agency.

FIXTURES: Items affixed to buildings or land, usually in such a way that they cannot be moved without damage to themselves or the property; such as fences, plumbing, electrical fixtures, trees, etc.

FORECLOSURE: Procedure where property pledged for security for a debt is sold to pay the debt in the event of default in payment and terms.

GRADUATED LEASE: A lease which provides for rental adjustments, often based upon future determination or the cost of living index; used for the most part in long term leases.

GROSS INCOME: Total income from property before any expenses are deducted.

HOMESTEAD: A declaration by the owner of a home that protects the home against judgments up to specified amounts, as provided by California Statutes.

HYPOTHECATE: To give a thing as security without giving up possession of it. To mortgage real property.

IMPOUND ACCOUNT: Monies held in trust by lender for payment of taxes and insurance.

INSTALLMENT NOTE: A note that provides for regular monthly payments to be paid on the date specified in the instrument.

INTANGIBLE VALUE: The goodwill or well advertised name of an established business.

INTERIM LOAN: A short term loan, usually for real estate improvements during the period of construction.

INTESTATE: A person who dies without having made a will.

JOINT TENANCY: Joint ownership by two or more persons with right of survivorship.

LAND CONTRACT: Same as Conditional Sales Contract.

LEASE: A contract between the owner of real property, called the lessor, and another person, called the lessee, covering conditions the lessee may occupy and use the property.

LEGACY: A gift of personal property by will.

LESSEE: One who contracts to rent property under a lease.

LESSOR: An owner who contracts into a lease with a tenant.

LEVERAGE: The use of a small amount of value to control a large amount of value.

LIEN: A charge or encumbrance upon the property for the payment of a debt.

LIQUIDATE: Disposal of property or assets or settlement of debts.

LIQUIDITY: The ability of property to be exchanged for cash.

LISTING: A contract between owner and broker, authorizing broker to sell the principal's property.

M.A.I.: Designates a person who is a member of the American Institute of Real Estate Appraisers.

MARKETABLE TITLE: A saleable title free of objectionable liens or encumbrances.

MARKET PRICE: The price a property will sell for in a given market.

MARKET VALUE: The price a buyer will pay and a seller will accept, both fully informed.

METES AND BOUNDS: A legal description used in describing boundary lines.

MORATORIUM: Temporary suspension of the enforcement of liability for debt.

MORTGAGE: An instrument by which property is hypothecated to secure the payment of a debt.

MORTGAGOR: One who borrows on his property and gives a mortgage as security.

MULTIPLE LISTING: A listing, taken by a member of an organization of brokers, whereby all its members have the opportunity to find a buyer.

NET LEASE: A lease requiring tenant to pay all or part of expenses in maintaining the property, in addition of stipulated rent.

NOTE: A written instrument acknowledging a debt and promising payment.

OBSOLESCENCE: Loss in value due to reduced usefulness or desirability of a structure.

OPEN LISTINGS: An authorization given by owner to real estate agent to sell his property; open listings may be given to more than one agent without liability, and only the one who secures a buyer on satisfactory terms gets paid a commission.

OPTION: A right given for a consideration to purchase or lease a property upon stipulated terms within a specified time.

PERCENTAGE LEASE: A lease on property where normally a minimum specified rent is paid or a percentage of gross receipts of the lessee is paid, whichever is higher.

PERSONAL PROPERTY: Property which is not real property.

PIGGY BACK: Property being carried by another.

PLANNED DEVELOPMENT: Five or more individually owned lots where one or more other parcels are owned in common or there are reciprocal rights in one or more other parcels. A subdivision.

PLAT: A map or plan of a specified parcel of land.

PLAT BOOK: A book showing lots and legal subdivisions of an area.

POWER OF ATTORNEY: An instrument authorizing a person to act as the agent of the person granting it.

PRINCIPAL: The employer of an agent.

PRORATION OF TAXES: To divide or prorate the taxes equally or proportionately to time of use.

PYRAMID: To build an estate by multiple acquisition of properties.

QUITCLAIM DEED: A deed used to remove clouds on title by relinquishing any right, title or interest that the grantor may have.

REALTOR: A real estate broker holding membership in a real estate board affiliated with the National Association of Realtors.

REDEMPTION: The buying back of one's property after it has been lost through foreclosure. Payment of delinquent taxes after sale to the state.

RIGHT OF SURVIVORSHIP: Right to acquire the interest of a deceased joint owner. Distinguishing characteristic of joint tenancy.

RIGHT-OF-WAY: A privilege given by the owner of a property to give another the right to pass over his land.

RIPARIAN RIGHTS: The right of a landowner to water on, under, or adjacent to his land.

SALES CONTRACT: A contract by which buyer and seller agree to terms of a sale.

SELLERS MARKET: More buyers than sellers.

SEPARATE PROPERTY: Property owned by husband or wife

which is not community property; property acquired by prior marriage or by a gift, will, or inheritance.

SEVERALTY OWNERSHIP: Owned by one person only. Sole ownership.

SHERIFF'S DEED: Deed given by court order in connection with the sale of a property to satisfy a judgment.

SPECIAL ASSESSMENT: Legal charge against real estate by public authority to pay cost of public improvements by which the property is benefited.

S.R.E.A.: Designates a person who is a member of Society of Real Estate Appraisers.

SUBJECT TO MORTGAGE: When a buyer takes title to real property "subject to mortgage", he is not responsible to the holder of the note. The original maker of the note is not released from the responsibility of the note and the most the buyer can lose in foreclosure is his equity in the property.

SUBLEASE: A lease given by a lessee.

SYNDICATE: Group of investors who invest in one or more properties, through a partnership, corporation, or trust.

TAKE-OUT COMMITMENT: Agreement by a lender to have available a long term loan over a specified time for construction work.

TAX SALE: A sale of property, usually at auction, for non-payment of taxes assessed against it.

TENANCY IN COMMON: Ownership by two or more persons who hold undivided interest without right or survivorship.

TENDER: An offer of money, usually in satisfaction of a claim or demand.

TENEMENTS: All rights in land which pass with conveyance of the land.

TESTATOR: A person who leaves a valid will at his death.

TIGHT MONEY: A condition in which demand for the use of money exceeds the available supply.

TITLE INSURANCE: Insurance written by a title company to protect the property owner against loss if title is imperfect.

TOPOGRAPHY: Character of the surface of land; topography may be level, rolling, or mountainous.

TOWNSHIP: A territorial subdivision six miles long, six miles wide and containing 36 sections. each one mile square.

TRUST DEED: An instrument which conveys legal title of a property to a trustee to be held pending fulfillment of an obligation; usually the repayment of a loan to a beneficiary (lender).

TRUSTEE: One who holds bare legal title to a property in trust for another to secure performance of an obligation.

TRUSTOR: The borrower of money secured by a deed of trust.

TURKEY: A property which total expenses exceeds its income. Something to eat at Thanksgiving time.

UNLAWFUL DETAINER: An action at law to evict a person or persons occupying real property unlawfully.

USURY: Interest rate on a loan in excess of that permitted by law.

VENDEE: A purchaser; buyer.

VENDOR: A seller.

VESTED: Bestowed upon someone or secured by someone; such as title to property.

WAIVE: To relinquish or abandon; to forego a right to enforce or require anything.

WRAP-AROUND MORTGAGE: A purchase money mortgage which is subordinate to, but includes the encumbrances to which it is subordinated.

ZONING: Act of city or county authorities specifying types of use for which property may be used in specific areas.

MONTHLY LOAN PAYMENT TABLE

This table shows the monthly payment required to pay off a $1,000 loan in various periods and at various interest rates. To find monthly payment required for larger denominations, multiply number in column corresponding to term and interest rate by number of thousands. Thus, the monthly payment on a $8,000 loan for 5 years at 10% would be $21.25 x 8 = $170.00.

Interest Rate	Number Of Years In Term					
	1	2	3	4	5	8
8.00%	86.99	45.23	31.34	24.42	20.28	14.14
8.25	87.11	45.35	31.46	24.54	20.40	14.27
8.50	87.22	45.46	31.57	24.65	20.52	14.40
8.75	87.34	45.58	31.69	24.77	20.64	14.53
9.00	87.46	45.69	31.80	24.89	20.76	14.66
9.25	87.57	45.80	31.92	25.01	20.88	14.79
9.50	87.69	45.92	32.04	25.13	21.01	14.92
9.75	87.80	46.03	32.15	25.25	21.13	15.05
10.00	87.92	46.15	32.27	25.37	21.25	15.18
10.25	88.04	46.27	32.39	25.49	21.38	15.31
10.50	88.15	46.38	32.51	25.61	21.50	15.45
10.75	88.27	46.50	32.63	25.73	21.62	15.58
11.00	88.39	46.61	32.74	25.85	21.75	15.71
11.25	88.50	46.73	32.86	25.97	21.87	15.85
11.50	88.62	46.85	32.98	26.09	22.00	15.98
11.75	88.74	46.96	33.10	26.22	22.12	16.12
12.00	88.85	47.08	33.22	26.34	22.25	16.26
12.50	89.09	47.31	33.46	26.58	22.50	16.53
13.00	89.32	47.55	33.70	26.83	22.76	16.81

MONTHLY LOAN PAYMENT TABLE

Monthly payment required on a $1,000 loan for 10 years at 12% would be $14.35. For larger denominations, multiply number in column by the number of thousands in the loan.

Interest Rate	Number Of Years In Term					
	10	12	15	20	25	30
8.00%	12.14	10.83	9.56	8.37	7.72	7.34
8.25	12.27	10.97	9.71	8.53	7.89	7.52
8.50	12.40	11.11	9.85	8.68	8.06	7.69
8.75	12.54	11.24	10.00	8.84	8.23	7.87
9.00	12.67	11.39	10.15	9.00	8.40	8.05
9.25	12.81	11.53	10.30	9.16	8.57	8.23
9.50	12.94	11.67	10.45	9.33	8.74	8.41
9.75	13.08	11.81	10.60	9.49	8.92	8.60
10.00	13.22	11.96	10.75	9.66	9.09	8.78
10.25	13.36	12.10	10.90	9.82	9.27	8.97
10.50	13.50	12.25	11.06	9.99	9.45	9.15
10.75	13.64	12.39	11.21	10.16	9.63	9.34
11.00	13.78	12.54	11.37	10.33	9.81	9.53
11.25	13.92	12.69	11.53	10.50	9.99	9.72
11.50	14.06	12.84	11.69	10.67	10.17	9.91
11.75	14.21	12.99	11.85	10.84	10.35	10.10
12.00	14.35	13.14	12.01	11.02	10.54	10.29
12.50	14.64	13.44	12.33	11.37	10.91	10.68
13.00	14.94	13.75	12.66	11.72	11.28	11.07

BOOK II

THE MOST EXCITING BUSINESS IN THE ENTIRE UNIVERSE

You can create a national...even a world-wide business...almost overnight. It doesn't require huge amounts of capital...and it's just about the last frontier for an enterprising "little guy". In no other business have so many started with so little and became rich.

It's called the "direct reply business," or in more common terms, the mail order business. You know some of the household names: Sears and Roebuck, Montgomery Wards, and Sunset House, just to mention a few. They are all part of a vast multi-billion dollar empire that continues to profit from offering the public services, products, or information through the mail.

Why is this such a dynamic, growing business? Because it offers convenience to the public. Customer's can simply dial a toll free number, or browse through a magazine or catalogue and order by mail, instead of hastling with crowds and traffic at the shopping center. Because for the mail order operator it's efficient; he does not have to pay employees for hanging around during slack hours, also handling cost are reduced, and thus lower prices can be offered to customers. Most products go through many distribution channels before finally reaching the consumer. Wholesalers, jobbers, and distributors all mark up the product to cover high costs, plus a profit; then the retailer ups the price further to cover the costs of prime real estate, fixtures, and employees. To avoid these expenses, more and more products are being sold everyday by direct reply.

You can compete with the retail giants because you won't have any middlemen to sipher your profits. Unlike other businesses, starting small in mail order is not a handicap. Low overhead and direct control work for you. Plus, you have no credit risk because it's basically a cash business. No large inventory nor rent for a warehouse or shop is required. You can start from a small desk in your own home in your spare time.

Of course, later on when your company has developed, you can enjoy some of the niceties of a thriving large business: with secretaries, executive restrooms, etc. But until you reach the "big time," keep your overhead as low as possible. This will help to insure your future success. Just imagine...financial independence and all the wonderful freedom it brings. You can plan your whole day...just as you want it. No more being strapped to a time card or to a monotonous routine.

What I enjoy most out of the freedom I've attained in my direct reply business is watching all the 8-to 5-ers getting up day after day with the dread of going to work...at a job they don't enjoy...for a boss they can't stand, and knowing that I am responsible only to myself. I work when I please and where I please, and can work, more or less, as much as I want, depending on how much money I wish to make. And that my friend is what I want you to attain.

FREEDOM FOR LIFE

Imagine yourself opening envelopes daily stuffed with checks and money orders along with requests for your products. Sounds exciting, doesn't it? Don't quit your current job yet, though. In the beginning you'll start part-time while maintaining your normal full time hours. Your current employment is important because it will help enable you to finance your operations. Later on, as your business begins to prosper and become self sufficient, you can consider quitting your job and putting your full time efforts into your new enterprise.

As your business grows, you can consider hiring employees to handle opening mail, banking, and processing your orders. Initially, however, it is crucial to the success of your business to keep overhead to an absolute minimum and to do this type of work yourself. This will serve to give you expertise in overall operation, making it easier to show someone else how to do necessary functions when the time comes.

The direct reply business is real, and a part of it is available to you. It's a multi-billion dollar business that's getting bigger by the day. The media continues to bombard the public with offereings of education, weight loss, health and diet, and various other forms of self improvement...all through the mail. It is my intention to help you find your own niche in this most desirable business.

Why is this business so desirable? Because you make your own hours; you are your own boss; you can work at home; and you can start on a shoestring.

Before we get started, I must state that your success will depend on some very basic principles. You must have the determination to succeed and the willingness to use common sense. I also suggest you use the formulated steps in the following chapters as a guide. If you're to take a chance and to believe in yourself, you will succeed.

GETTING STARTED

A journey of a thousand miles cannot be accomplished without taking the first step. As a novice mail order operator you would do well to begin with one product, than later develop a full line as you acquire expertise. The big mail order operators started this way...you should too! Remember, you had to learn to walk before you could eventually run!

Your first step is to establish a permanent mailing address which can handle a large volume of mail. If you already have a stable address, use it, or if you don't plan to move in the near future, use your home address. Better yet, rent a box at your local post office, if it is conveniently located. A post office box is handy in case you move later on. It is permanent and it will enable you to mail out orders while you are picking up the incoming mail.

DEVELOPING A COMPANY NAME

Selecting a company name, other than your own last name, will require you to register a ficticious name statement at the county clerk's office. This registration is necessary to protect the general public against fraud. If a consumer is cheated by an unscrupulous operator, it is possible to trace the owner of the ficticious name. (There are a few illegal operators around who attempt to bilk the public, but for the most part mail order operators, especially successful ones, offer quality products they stand behind). When you register your company name, a minimal registration fee is required along with various forms the county clerk will supply.

When choosing a name, try to use a simple, descriptive title which represents the products you plan to develop. Be careful of making your title overly specific, such as "Richman Jewels," which associates you only with jewels. Later on, in your direct reply profession, you may decide to market other products unrelated to jewels or even to publish a book. Therefore, select a more general name, which can include these possibilities. Also choose an name that is easy to remember and easy to pronounce, like "Van-Go Gifts," not "Charles Van Gogh Elongated Keepsakes ."

Try to pick a name that's original. It may happen that another company will notify you that you are using their name. Later, when you are well established, some new upstart company may be in conflict with your name, and you will have to notify him of the similarity. It's much easier for the less established company to change its name than to spend eons battling in court.

THE DIRECT REPLY BUSINESS DEFINED

Essentially, the direct reply business involves selling products to customers whom one never sees personally. Ads are placed in various media, such as tv, radio, and magazines, then products are mailed to those who respond to them. There is a direct connection between the business and the customer; no middleman is involved.

On other occassions you may want to use the indirect approach, which entails an extra step in the total operation. Instead of advertising for orders directly, you advertise to stimulate inquiries, then send your sales material directly to the inquirer to close the sale. This indirect approach is generally used for higher priced items where more information about the product is required to close the sale and sufficient space isn't available in a paid advertisement.

WHAT TO SELL

The most difficult decision you'll have to make is deciding what to sell. I will offer you some ideas to assist in determining that, but in general, what you sell should be a better service, information, or even a lower priced product than what someone else is selling. In the beginning you should spend your time researching the products which are advertised in various magazines and tabloids that are popular among mail order operators; such as the National Enquirer, Popular Mechanics, Salesman magazines, etc. Typically, what is advertised month after month are the proven, successful products. If they weren't successful, the operator wouldn't continue to invest in expensive advertising to promote them.

PRODUCT SELECTION

In general terms, anything offered for sale can be categorized as (a) a product, (b) a service, or (c) information. Products are basically merchandise, everyday items that are normally available at most local stores, like clothing, toilet paper, and soap. They are readily available to the consumer because they are heavily used by the insatiable public. And there are plenty of suppliers who are in the business to make a profit by supplying these needs. Services may include loans by mail, insurance, repair work of all types, film development, and packaging. Information can be represented by books, correspondence schools, and self-improvement courses. How-to books, including self improvement techniques, have always been highly saleable and classically successful in the mail order industry.

Inventing a product or service, or writing a book is obviously for those of a creative nature. For everyone else, products are available through other wholesalers. These wholesalers have catalogues of various products which are available at wholesale prices to you for resale to the public. You'll see these wholesale representatives advertised when you begin researching magazine publications.

To help you decide what to sell, make a list of activities you enjoy and/or do better than other people. Are you a great poker player or gambler? Do you know more about dieting and exercise than the average person? What about the opposite sex...do you feel you're a great lover? How about blending your terrific sence of humor with your grandmother's proven recipes to create the "Erotic Cookbook?"

For more ideas, take a look at the current direct reply ads and see what others are selling. You'll find that memory courses, hypnotism made easy, and dieting and health care are very big time and have sold successfully for many years. If you're a television fan and you live near a large city, you've probably seen tv ads promoting bartender schools, truck driving schools, and secretarial courses. These offerings are samples of other direct reply businesses which are selling training for professional careers.

Many successful direct reply businesses have been built on these topics...and there is plenty of room for you. Take some of the ideas offered both here and in various magazines and create your own list. Once you have your list, begin narrowing down your potential products to a few definite prospects. Now, play around with them. Begin outlining selling features for each. You don't have to have a product to sell. You can sell an idea, a plan for wealth or health, or a way of doing something better, faster or cheaper than anyone else.

The secret to success in mail order is "TO SELL WHAT EVERYONE ELSE IS SELLING." To be innovative and to develop the first "hula-hoop" or "pet rock" is extremely risky and occassionally will be successful for the short term, but we are concerned with proven products that sell year after year, and I want you to have a lifetime income, not a quick splash in the pan.

The most successful mail order operators, including myself, sell some sort of product, service, or information that they know is wanted by the public. Therefore, the thing to do is sell items that are similar to what everyone else is selling. It is much easier to sell items that the public already has a need for, than to try to create that need.

We all want to be successful, to make more money, to be more attractive to the opposite sex, to be positive thinkers and to have the respect of others. The general public will readily pay for products, services, or information which offers to help them attain any of these.

What about activities, hobbies, or anything you enjoy doing. Maybe you're a great lover, or a gourmet cook, a travel freak. Some of us are master mechanics, or builders of cages for elusive flying turtles. (What a crazy idea). Whatever the case, you don't have to be an expert, just keep adding to the list and watch it expand. Once you begin outlining and writing on your chosen subject, you'll be surprised how much you do know. Let your imagination ramble on, perhaps you would like to write about your ten favorite gripes. Or, how about how people exploit welfare and unemployment, or card cheaters, crime in the streets, whatever!

There are many people in the United States today who would really like to know how best to invest $1,000 to $10,000. Savings, treasury bills stocks, second mortgages? What about mutual funds or savings bonds? The little guy in America is in a tizzy as to where to invest these sums of money. Someone ought to write a book to satisfy this demand throughout the country. Why don't you?

How about a book about the crazy ways some people earn a living. Have you ever noticed ads for a "remailing service?" This is a person whom you mail your outgoing correspondence to. He then mails it from his address at 25¢ per letter. This service gives the customer a post mark from somewhere other than the city he actually lives in. Apparently, it is utilized by persons who would rather not have others know where they are living. You know the type, "alimony skippers," people hiding from bill collectors, etc. This is just one example. There are hundreds of other unusual occupations that those with more mundane jobs would enjoy reading about.

Unlimited possibilities are yours. Maybe you know how to operate a restaurant? How about becoming a bartender? Jack Tiano of American Bartender Schools has a complete training course he advertises on prime-time television in both New York and Los Angeles. You can train people to be bartenders through the mail.

Weight loss and dieting are a very big business. Winn's "super-belt" sold for years nationally from tv ads at $9.95. It is simply an elastic belt which fits around your waist and makes you look trim.

Nutrition and cooking are also a tremendous business. Next time you're in a bookstore, take note of the large section delegated to cookbooks. Believe me, there is a reason for it...cookbooks sell very well.

The secret then, in determining the success of a product, is to sell what has already been proven. Sell what everyone else is selling. That is a product you have developed that is the same as, or similar to, what everyone else is selling.

Successful direct reply operators know what products are being sold profitably because they see the same ads over and over again for an extended period of time. Creativity and innovation, good qualities to have in almost any type of business, are not usually profitable, especially for unseasoned operators in the mail order business.

To determine what is being sold successfully, you'll have to do some research at your local library. Get back issues of various leading magazines and newspapers. Point out interesting ads of similar products to yours in the latest issues, then start looking in the same magazines or newspapers of back issues until you find the same or similar ad by the same operator. When the same ad appears repetively, you can rest assured that the product being advertised is successful.

Stay with the winners, those proven sellers you see being advertised over the years. If you have an entirely new idea, shelve it for the time being until you gain some insight and experience. It is much easier to offer products, services, or information that the public already demands and needs, than to try and create that need.

DEVELOPMENT OF AN IDEA

At this point you should have some idea of what you might successfully sell to the mass market of consumers. Since my specialty is publishing self-improvement books, I now plan to assist you in developing your own book to sell by direct reply.

I truly feel that a book, designed in the format of a self-improvement (how-to) manual, is the ideal item to sell by mail order for the following reasons. A book can be produced economically, for less than a dollar a piece, allowing it to be marked up and priced to ten dollars, which is an ideal direct reply price. Furthermore, if the book is good enough, it can be sold retail in 30,000 book outlets throughout the United States. Also, a book can be easily packaged and mailed more economically than other bulkier products.

HOW TO WRITE A BOOK

When you sell an interested reader a book, you don't sell ten ounces of glue and paper...you frequently open hidden doors to a new and wonderful life. As a novelist, one can offer pain and love, perhaps some humor, and maybe even a chuckle or two. A writing tradesman can outline the foundation of a new and stimulating career. While both types of writers are communicating a passage of ideas...from the maker to the reader.

Whether you know it or not, everybody is an expert on something! As long as you know more about a particular subject that the average person, you can be considered an expert to a certain degree, and the hungry-for-knowledge public will pay well to gain your expertise on a subject that interests them.

Although I have written three books in the past two years on the subject of real estate, I do not consider myself an expert on the subject. However, my friends and many of my readers do because I know more about it than they do. Many of my peers who are equally or even more educated than myself in real estate, I'm sure, could teach me a few things, but I don't write for them. Instead, I am interested in passing on what I have learned to the average layman, those who are curious but don't know much about the subject.

Before you begin writing about your chosen subject, you will want to research it to gain further information. Doing this will make you even more of an expert. After you finish your book and publish it, you will then be considered an expert by your readers. Some may criticize what you have to say, but for the most part you will be educating those who have little knowledge of your subject.

ORGANIZATION

In a lot of cases, the subject you've chosen has been entertaining your thoughts for quite a while, and you've compiled various notes and shoved them away in a drawer for later use. Your procedure now is to begin organizing that material into an outline.

An outline begins with your basic title and various subheadings for chapters. To start, write each subheading at the top of a standard piece of paper. Add other sheets as you think of more. When something comes to you about your subject, write the details beneath the appropriate subheadings. Continue adding new thoughts, and soon more and more material will develop beneath your main headings which eventually will be expanded into complete chapters.

The important thing is to start writing. Don't bother searching for that perfect first word at the beginning of a paragraph. You can later improve and refine your thoughts. Write about whatever appeals to you at the time. If you can't start at the beginning, start somewhere else, but start! Most writers agree that you shouldn't stop writing just because you've reached a logical break, like the end of a chapter. Either write more, or stop short. Then, when you continue later on, it will be easier for you to pick up the flow where you left off, rather than having to start entirely anew.

If by chance you do get "writer's block," go back over what you've written and begin revising. You'll find you can add more refining and fill in the gaps this way.

After you have compiled numerous pages with the major thoughts as chapter headings, begin filling in the gaps so your work flows smoothly from subject to subject. Double space all your typing so that your editor will have plenty of room for corrections and notations. Avoid typing over a mistake so that the final draft won't include the error. Penciling in your corrections and notations is more flexible than any other method.

EDITING

Remember, you don't need a Ph.D. in English Composition to be a successful writer. You simply need to communicate your ideas and then find an editor to refine your work. If you were an "A" student in English grammar, you may not need an editor, but if you're like me, you should have someone competent in grammar mark up your final draft. Also, it might be advisable for you to have someone else proofread your final draft after editing, just to be safe.

PUBLISHING

The book you are currently reading is my third book published in the last two years. Five years ago, if anyone had told me that I would have even one published book at this time, I would have told them they were crazy. My interest in writing began when I read a friend of mine's pamphlet on how to write your own book. It was so good that I thought it should be selling in bookstores nationwide. At the time, he was selling it strictly by mail order, with only marginal success. I tried to buy half interest in it with hopes of developing a national market for it. Unfortunately, he didn't wish to sell, and I was left thinking about ideas presented to me in its excellent contents.

Needless to say, I decided to take his advice and write my own book. But what was I to write about? Since real estate had become my profession, both working for others and investing on my own, the obvious decision was to write about it. I prepared a 67 page pamphlet, had it printed and bound, and began selling it by mail order. When my friends inquired about my recent doings, I would respond by showing them my pamphlet. I was really impressed with their responses and decided to take my new writing career a further step.

I visited my local Walden bookstore and asked the manager if she would be interested in placing my pamphlet for sale in her store. Her response was, that since it was a pamphlet, not really a book with a title on the spine, it would be difficult for her to sell. However, if I made it into a book with more of a catchy title on the spine she would place it on consignment, since real estate books always did well in her store.

Within three weeks I made all the necessary changes in binding and title and placed ten copies on consignment in the local Walden bookstore. Since then I have sold 30,000 copies of one title, ten thousand of another, and have sold the publishing rights for one title to a firm in Canada.

Publishing means "to make available to the public, or reveal." Typically in the book business, large publishing houses like McGraw Hill, Random House, and Doubleday take a finished manuscript from an author and do everything necessary to produce a finished book ready for sale at your local bookstore. Particular instances may vary slightly, but the following steps usually transpire between a free lance writer and a publisher. A finished manuscript is sent to the publisher for approval of sale. If accepted, a contract is proposed by the publisher. The publisher agrees to edit, print, bind and distribute an arbitrary number of copies. In return, the author will receive a royalty on every copy sold. The royalty can vary from 4% to 15% of the selling price of the book, depending on which printing the book is in and how well known the author is. The first printing of a book is normally the costliest, as printing plates and art work costs have to be absorbed. Additional printings usually offer the author a higher percentage royalty as publishing costs are not as substantial as the initial printing.

Today, a typical paperback sells for about $2.50. The retail bookstore will receive about 40% of the gross selling price, or $1.00. The wholesale book distributor will receive about 10% for distributing it. The remaining 50% goes to the publisher, of which the author will receive a royalty of 4 to 15%.

Since you won't be soliciting for a publisher but will be your own publisher, the following will become your responsibility. You will need to write or call R.R. Bowker Company, 1180 Avenue of the Americas, New York, NY 10036, to register your title for an ISBN (International Standard Book Number). An

ISBN is a registered code number assigned to you, the publisher, which identifies your title among the millions of others. Bookstores and distributors use this number for ordering purposes. Bowker will assign you this number free of charge, and will also publish your title, along with a brief description, in Books In Print, which is a standard guide used by bookstores to locate titles and authors requested by customers.

Once you acquire your ISBN, you can begin typesetting procedures. Typesetting is arranging your final manuscript into final graphic form wherein both right hand and left hand margins are justified, or blocked, and a particular style of type is used. Typesetting is done today either by hand or photographic process wherein your words are projected onto a thin metal plate, and transferred to paper. You can simply take your manuscript to a reputable printer and he can describe and do all the necessary processes. Once the contents and cover are printed, you can also arrange for book binding through your printer.

Once the finished book has been bound, you will need to sent two copies, along with $10, to the Library of Congress, Copyright Office, Washington, D.C. 20559. This will ensure you that no one can copy your work without legal ramifications. In fact, write in advance so that you will have all the necessary forms ready to mail when your book is finished.

BOOK DESIGN

Eventually your book may be offered for sale in bookstores. In order for it to sell successfully at the retail level, it must have an appealing cover. I can't really stress this point enough. You will be competing with from 10,000 to 150,000 other various titles in any particular store, and your book cover has to have something special in order to catch a customer's eye.

Book buyers who work for large retailing chains look at the cover, if it is appealing they look further into the contents. The public does the same thing. If a cover attracts them, they will pick up the book and begin browsing through its contents. If your book looks non-professional or if the design is in poor taste, chances are your book won't sell at the retail level.

Begin with a short, descriptive title that is easy to remember. The front cover should include only the title, author's name, a brief testimonial, and an ISBN. The back cover may be used for a review of your book and your address for anyone who wishes to purchase additional copies.

The spine of the book must include the title and the author's name. This will allow bookstores to place your books spine out on their shelves.

As far as the contents, design your text so that it is well organized and easy to read. Selecting a large type will make it easier for your reader to peruse your text.

COSTS RELATED TO PUBLISHING

A difficult decision you will be faced with is how many books you should have printed and bound? The initial printing will always be the most expensive on a per book basis because of the design work, typesetting, and layout work required. In 1976, the 67 page pamphlet I wrote cost 80¢ a book for a printing of 500 copies, or a total of $400. The second printing of that particular edition cost 36¢ a piece for 5,000 copies. The cost was substantially less because layout and typesetting costs had been absorbed the first time and also a larger number of books were printed this time.

It is best to be conservative and only print about 500 copies initially. Later on, you can arrange for a larger printing when you're sure your books are going to sell.

Typesetting costs are separate from printing and binding costs, and can vary substantially depending on the size of the pages and who is doing the job. Professional typesetters usually charge from $4 to $10 per page. You could simply type out all your finished pages on a standard typewriter and have them reproduced without professional typesetting. However, I wouldn't recommend this method as it looks very non-professional and it would be difficult for your books to sell at the retail level without being typeset.

ADVERTISING

Professional advertising agencies can set up and create all your advertising. They in turn will charge you 15% of all monies you spend in the various media to promote your products. However, when you're a small business person just starting out, it is often difficult to get a good agency to work for you, since you won't be spending much money on advertising at first. Therefore, it is best to become your own ad agency, design and insert your own ads and save that 15%. The 15% you save by becoming your own ad agency begins to be quite substantial later when you're spending thousands in advertising.

To establish yourself as an advertising agency, select a company name that is different from your direct reply company name. Often ad agencies use names like "Richardson & Associates" or "Windmark Agency." (It is quite common to use "associates" when describing an advertising agency.) Besides a name for your ad agency, you'll also need a separate checking account under your agency name to use for payment of all your advertising.

The 15% the advertising agencies earn is basically a 15% discount allowed by the various forms of media. The general public pays a full rate to advertise, however, recognized ad agencies receive a 15% discount on all insertion orders. To earn that 15% discount on all your advertising, simply develop an agency name, checking account, and send in all your insertion orders on ad agency forms which you can have printed for yourself from the sample that follows. If you have any doubts, consult other mail order operators or ad agencies for advice as to the best medium to use for your particular products.

Once you've been recognized as an ad agency, you can then begin establishing credit with the various publications you advertise in. In most cases, the first ads you place will require payment in advance along with the insertion order. Later on, after you have run a few ads and are better known, you'll be able to get credit terms allowing you to pay after the ad has run. This will enable you to pay for the ad with revenues generated from sales that result from the ad. Obviously it's better business to avoid paying expenses out of your own pocket so far in advance. Establishing credit and paying for advertising after it has run will allow you to do this.

SAMPLE AGENCY FORM

Order Blank For Publications

ORDER NO. _____

Date _____

☐ If checked here this is a SPACE RESERVATION

Advertiser ___ JWP

Product _____ Book _____

☒ If checked here this is a FIRM SPACE ORDER and
BINDING unless cancelled before closing date*

Contract Year _____

Discount Level _____

☐ If checked here this is CANCELLATION

or change of: _____

To the publisher of:

Edition: (specify) National ___

Regional ___

ISSUE DATE   SPACE   FREQUENCY   RATE

(COPY)

Position

Less agency commission 15% on gross
Cash discount   on net

Additional Instructions:

Mail all invoices to:

Copy instructions & material ☐ to follow   ☐ herewith

Address all other correspondence to:

_____

_____
(Authorized Signature)

WHEN & WHERE TO ADVERTISE

Determining where to place your advertising will require some research on your part as to where your competition has been selling similar products. You should advertise only in a medium which is appealing to those consumers who will have an interest in your product. Assume you're selling a nutritional cookbook. Obviously, you wouldn't want to advertise in magazines like Motor Trend or Popular Mechanics. Instead, you'd choose Family Circle, Good Housekeeping, or any of the popular women's magazines. If you were selling a car repair manual, then publications geared to mechanically inclined men would be appropriate for your advertising.

Begin researching publications you feel would be suitable for your particular product. Locate ads that describe products similar to yours. Then, go to the library and look up back issues of the same publications and search for the same ads you found in the current issue. If that particular operator has continued to advertise in that publication, then you can rest assured that that ad was profitable; otherwise that operator wouldn't have continued to run it in that magazine.

Simply locating one ad in any one magazine doesn't mean anything. That one-time ad may have been a test to see if it would be profitable. You need to see the ads repeated by the same advertiser to determine if it has been successful in that particular magazine.

As a general rule of thumb, the summer months and holiday periods are the slowest time of the year for mail order selling. Unless you have seasonal products, like Christmas gifts, or you're selling charter flights for summer vacations, avoid advertising these seasonal times of the year. Here is a general ranking from best to worst as to which months are best for mail order selling. January, February, March, October, November, September, August, April and May. December is excellent if you're selling gift items, questionable for other offers.

WHEN TO USE CLASSIFIED ADS

Classified advertising, unlike display advertising, is sold by the word and classified under specific headings. All classified ads are set in the same type and all look alike, lacking prominence among the numerous other ads. A prospect who reads your ad is usually looking for something specific under a certain column heading.

Classified ads are most effective when the product you're selling is priced at $3.00 or less and sold directly, or when you're advertising to arouse interest, which will be followed up with sales literature. When a classified ad is used to pull immediate sales, the product must be familar enough to the prospect to require little descriptive copy in order to sell it successfully, such as a book entitled "Nutrition, Diet, and Exercise-A Complete Do-it-yourself Guide." If a product is priced higher than $3.00, it will require more descriptive copy in order to pull enough orders to make the ad practical.

Classified ads usually do not experience a fall off in sales from running month-to-month consecutively as do display ads. This occurs because only a small percentage of readers see the small classified ad and the readership continually changes. Whereas a large display ad will begin to lose its pull if the ad continues to run month after month and the same readers see the ad.

WHEN TO USE DISPLAY ADS

Display advertising is basically any advertising which isn't classfied. It is paid for on a column inch basis, per full page, or half or quarter page. Display advertising is required when you want to sell directly to your prospects and the price of your product is more than $3 and less than $10. At a price above ten dollars, it is usually necessary to advertise for inquiries, then send off an appealing sales brochure with plenty of descriptive copy in order to sell your product successfully. Above ten dollars, much buyer resistance is encountered, so the prospect needs to read an elaborate sales message in order to satisfy his doubts and order your product.

Avoid running your display advertising in consective months in the same publications. Unlike classified advertising, over-exposure to your readers will cause a fall off in orders.

MAGAZINES vs. NEWSPAPERS

Magazines will always pull better than newspapers and offer a greater return on advertising expenditures. Magazines have a longer life and a more select readership and are passed on to other readers. Note all the back issues, especially of monthly magazines, which remain in barber shops and doctor's offices for customers and patients to read while waiting for their appointments.

Monthly magazines have the chief disadvantage of requiring you to place the ad six to eight weeks in advance of their sale dates. This requires the advertiser to wait six to eight weeks before orders start coming in. Weekly magazines usually have closing dates for advertising insertion orders of about three to four weeks in advance of their sale date.

Newspapers have the advantage of getting quick results for the advertiser as an ad can be placed a few days before the paper goes on the newstand. However, newspapers have the disadvantage of a short life and a broad range of readership. Newspapers are generally skimmed, then tossed into the trash. Because of their short life, most of the orders obtained will be received during the first two weeks after the ad appears, with the balance coming in the third week. With magazines, orders often continue trickling in up to a year after the publication date.

MAIL ORDER MAGAZINES

Publishers of magazines are aware of social status, financial capability, age and sex. Their publications are aimed at specific market segments. Thus, it is up to you to select the specific publications which are designed for those who might be interested in your product.

The following list of magazines has been compiled to assist

you in identifying their type of readership and type of merchandise most successfully advertised in them.

Space doesn't allow me to print all the publications available and their respective circulations. See your librarian for up-to-date publications under "Standard Rate and Data."

WOMEN READERS/Higher priced items

Ladies Home Journal	Better Homes & Gardens
Cosmopolitan	Sunset
Harper's Bazaar	Parents Magazine
Vogue	Good Housekeeping
Glamour	Mademoiselle
House Beautiful	House & Garden

WOMEN READERS/mass market products

McCall's Magazine
MacFaddens Womens Group
True Story
Photoplay
True Confessions
Complete Women's Group
Modern Romances
Secret Romance

WOMEN READERS/family magazines

Family Circle
Women's Day
Family Weekly
Sunday
Grit

MALE READERSHIP with a sophisticated flair

Playboy
Qui
Penthouse

MALE READERSHIP/mass market

True
Argosy
Complete Men's Group

MALE READERSHIP/Business & Finance
Fortune
Business Week
Baron's Weekly
Nation's Business
Free Enterprise

MALE READERSHIP/Mechanically inclined
Popular Mechanics
Popular Science Monthly
Mechanics Illustrated

Male readership/Sportsmen
Outdoor Life
Sports Illustrated
Field & Stream
Sports Afield

MALE READERSHIP/Newsworthy
Time
Newsweek
U.S. News & World Report
National Observer

MALE READERSHIP/Literary Man
The Atlantic
Saturday Review
Harper's
Writer's Digest

MALE READERSHIP/Specialty Salesman and Business
Opportunities
Money
Specialty Salesmen
Salesmen Opportunity
Money Making Opportunities
Income Opportunties
Spare Time

ADVERTISING FOR INQUIRIES

If you decide to advertise for inquiries only either because of your advertising budget or because the cost of your product is above ten dollars, then all you'll need is an eye catching headline and some well chosen copy to stimulate curiosity. However, this method entails closing only a certain percentage of those who respond to your advertisement. The problem arises when some of those inquiring are not truly qualified prospects. To ward off some of the free loaders who have no intention of ordering from your offer no matter how good it is, you can charge a small fee instead of offering completely free details.

Tests have shown that when free details are offered and 100 inquiries are answered with a good sales message, from 10 to 15% of these inquiries will be converted into orders. Whereas when the details offered cost 25¢ to the inquirer, total inquiries will drop one third, but the closing percentage of those who inquired goes up to between 35 and 40%.

Since the cost of circulars and postage have become so important, it would be wise to determine which method is best for your product. What good are hundreds of inquiries if they don't return a good profit?

DIRECT Vs. INDIRECT APPROACH

Generally speaking, there are two types of mail order ads: one makes a complete sale which I have been referring to as "direct reply;" the other arouses inquiries to the point that he writes for more information wherein the burden of closing the sale rest with the mailing piece that follows. The latter approach I have been referring to as the "Indirect reply method." The direct reply approach has the advantage of saving time, effort, and the expense of follow up sales material. However, the direct reply approach requires more advertising space than an inquiry ad, and for the same reason would cost more. The prospect who would send money for a product without seeing it first, to a company he knows nothing about, has to be convinced beyond a reasonable doubt that he is getting what he wants and good value.

Display advertising covering a large space is frequently used for items being sold by the direct reply approach priced at ten dollars or less. This is especially effective when more than one item is being offered and they are all of the same category and you are using a publication which is read by a specific group interested in that field. In this case a large ad would be broken up into individual units, each devoted to a different item. For example, one might have a full page ad running in business week advertising three books relating to the field of finance and real estate.

The indirect approach, advertising for inquiries, is ideal for higher priced items above ten dollars. Because you need adequate space to close a sale to convince a prospect to send money through the mail. This method can be used with classified ads or display advertising to stimulate inquiries by an attention-getting-headline or illustration, along with some well chosen words. This method allows you two options. You can advertise for free details, or you can charge a small amount for further information. By charging ten or twenty five cents, instead of offering free details, you eliminate some of the free-loaders who have no intention of ordering.

PRICING

After you have decided what to sell, you must determine at what price it will sell successfully. In the direct reply approach, the general rule of thumb is that the selling price should be at least *three to five times* your actual cost. Actual cost is defined as; the cost of the product, the cost of packaging including materials and labor, and the cost of postage. A three to five mark up ratio is required due to the use of expensive display advertising space used in the direct approach.

Furthermore, when the direct approach is used, the selling price of the items being sold should be in the range of $3 to $10. At a price above $10, display advertising space isn't sufficient enought to properly describe these more expensive products. Items above $10 are successfully sold through the indirect approach whereas an elaborate three or four page sales brochure can be sent to an inquiring customer.

Typically in the mail order business, the more costly the product, the more space the seller requires in order to sell his product successfully. An example can be given by a gentleman called Benson Barrett, who has been selling a professional writing course over the past twenty years. His advertising varies from a one-third page to full page display ads offering free details. If you send for the details, you receive a ton of sales material along with testimonials assuring the prospects of Barrett's success with his students. The course is fifty dollars. Should you not buy after receiving the sales material, a follow up brochure is sent two weeks later again requesting your fifty dollars. Because the price is high, much selling material is required to get the potential customer to part with his money.

When using the indirect approach, it is necessary to price your item at *eight to ten times* your exact product cost. For example, if you're selling a book which costs you 80¢ to produce, your selling price should be at least $6.40, but not more than $8.00. This pricing structure varies from the direct reply approach, because of all the additional costs of sales brochures and of handling and postage. The exact product cost is only the cost to acquire or manufacture it, not the additional costs of a sale brochure, handling and postage.

Unlike the direct reply approach, the indirect approach will only close a marginal number of inquiries. To be successful you will need a minimum of 8% of your inquirers ordering your product. If you have a very good sales letter that closes effectively, you can expect 10 to 15% return in orders from inquiries. Due to the marginal percentage of returns and the additional costs of sales brochure and handling requires that the indirect approach selling price be eight to ten times your exact product cost.

See the following examples of costs related to both the direct and indirect approach.

COSTS RELATED TO INDIRECT APPROACH

Figures based on 1,000 inquiries, 10% purchasing product at $8 each.

Sales from 1,000 inquiries x 10% equals 100 x $8 equals <u>$800</u> gross sales

Costs:

Advertising	$50
Cost of books (100 x 80)	$80
Cost of 2-envelopes & sales brochure (1,000 x 10¢)	$100
Cost of book envelope (100 x 5¢)	$5
Cost of postage of books sent (100 x 48¢)	$48
Cost of postage sales brochure (1,000 x 15¢)	$150
Total costs	$433
Net profit	$367

Costs related to direct approach (Heading)

Sales from 100 orders at $8 each equals $800 gross sales

Costs:

Advertising	$250
Postage (100 x 48¢)	$48
Book envelopes (100 x 5¢)	$5
Cost of books (100 x 80¢)	$80
Total costs	$383
Net profit	$417

Note that in the direct approach the advertising cost will always be higher because much more space is purchased in the media. Note also that costs for mailing of sales brochures and envelopes are not required in the direct approach.

WRITING THE AD

The following principles constitute the basics for a good ad...whether its a display ad, classified, or a sales brochure.
Gain the ATTENTION of the reader. This is the most important principle in advertising. If you don't get the reader's attention, obviously, he will not read your ad. Attention of the reader can be gained by illustrations or large headings with display advertising. In classified advertising, the ad is already placed under a specific heading, like Business Opportunities, or Hobbies, etc. Here, your first two words are in capitals to gain attention as well as to convey your actual message, something like "Wealth and Financial Independence" or "Nude Presidents."
Gain the INTEREST of the reader. Interest can be gained by offering a promise or a benefit of something. This is truly the meat of your ad and should be worded very carefully. Use short crisp sentences and persuasive language. To make your ad more exciting use active verbs. In the following example a benefit is offered to gain interest. "Financial Security can be acquired by writing information in your spare time." Everyone wants financial security and I have just promised it...by writing in your spare time.
A DESCRIPTION is required once you have the attention and interest of the reader in order to convert him to a customer. Such as, "A complete do-it-yourself guide to home improvement" or a "priceless manual for appraising antiques." Your description must be as tantalizing and exciting as you can possibly make it without exploiting the truth. If you're using display advertising and requesting a direct reply, then your description must be thorough enough so the customer isn't left with any questions about the merchandise. Under classified advertising a description isn't necessary, as your sales letter will describe your item in detail.

After the description, a CALL TO ACTION is required in order to get potential customer to respond to your promotion. "Write today" or "Rush," is generally adequate, followed by your address where he can reply to.

The last and one of the most significant principles in writing your ad is to include a GUARANTEE. I know for a fact that a guarantee increases sales substantially, so much in fact that the increase in sales completely outweighs any returns you'll have to make to unsatisfied customers.

KEYING THE AD

Keying the ad is very important as it tells you which particular ad your customer is responding to. Once you begin to advertise in more than one publication it becomes necessary to identify each ad so that you know which are successful in producing orders. Obviously, then, you will continue to use that ad in that publication as long as it continues profitable.

Here are some common methods for keying ads: Use a code number after your street address or post office box number, as in PO Box 2531-FE (FE would represent Free Enterprise Magazine.) FE-1 would mean Free Enterprise, January (the first month.) Use a code number after your address, such as PO Box 2531-Dept A, or room A, which would denote a particular magazine, and "A" would represent the first month, "B" the second month, etc.

MAILING LISTS

Mailing lists are rosters of names and addresses compiled by mail order brokers of people with various common characteristics. A compiled list may be of people in a given locale, or of a particular profession, or possibly of a political preference.

Mail order lists are compiled by other mail order houses and refer to names and addresses of people who have inquired about or bought some particular type of product through the mails. When this type of list is used, and sales brochures are sent to people who are proven mail order purchasers, results are always more productive than when mailing to a random list of names.

A house list is a list of names and addresses you have compiled of people who have inquired or purchased directly from you. This list will become invaluable to you as you continue to build it for future mailings of future products. You can also rent your own list to other brokers and mail order operators.

Ranking these lists as per effectiveness, your own house list will be most valuable to you. Second is a list of names of people who have purchased similar products by mail. Third would be a compiled list of people who have purchased anything by mail. Last in effectiveness would be a random list of people who simply have common characteristics which suggest they might consider your offer appealing.

If you were to compile a mailing list by simply taking names out of the phone book and then mail your sales brochure to these people, you might expect a 1% closing percentage in orders. Unfortunately, you would lose money at this rate.

In order to be successful with a list, you must know something about the quality of the names. Find out the dependability of the list and when it was compiled. If the list is too old, many other mailing houses may have used it, which means the people on the list are accustomed to "junk mail" and may be disregarding any new arrivals.

The following are certain qualities that you should look for in a profitable mailing list:

1. Are they the names of people who have previously purchased through the mails?
2. Is the list up to date and not overused?
3. Do the people have characteristics that indicate they may be interested in your products?

Before going head-over-heals, test a maximum of a thousand names by sending your sales material to these select few. If the results are positive, continue with your overall mailing campaign.

PREPARING A SALES BROCHURE

A sales brochure will only be required when you are using the indirect approach to mail order or when you plan to send off a sales letter to potential customers from a mailing list. In the direct approach a sales brochure is not required as you are advertising directly for orders and your ad serves the same purpose as a sales brochure.

For a sales letter to be effective, it has to incorporate the following important elements: a detailed explanation of the product, a list of benefits the customer will receive when he orders, testimonials (if available), a personal communicative style, and a guarantee. Your sales letter, although it is on a more personal level than a display ad, should still adhere to the same principles discussed earlier, that of ATTENTION, INTEREST, DESCRIPTION, and ACTION.

Begin analyzing your product. Write down each benefit to the consumer. Also list possible uses, and detail its construction. Note all these points in their order of importance. Take a look at other ads selling similar products and notice how they are written.

After you've compiled all the important points, begin elaborating on each point with enthusiasm. Get your customer excited, but be sincere. Your prospect will be enticed to believe in your product as you project the benefits he will receive from ordering.

Every message has a beginning, a middle, and an end. When writing a sales letter to follow up on the inquiries you advertised for, your beginning should be directed toward the ad which prompted the inquiry. This acts to disarm the prospect who doesn't want to be sold something he really doesn't need.

The body of your message should contain descriptive material associated with benefits that will interest the prospect. Tests have shown that a lengthy, descriptive letter out sells a brief letter. However, be careful not to ramble on with unimportant copy.

The conclusion of your message must include exact terms, simplified to avoid any confusion. Experience shows that orders will increase when postage is included in the quoted price. The average person isn't familiar with parcel post rates and will hesitate to guessing for fear of overpaying. I would also avoid any C.O.D. shipments as they only complicate matters.

Orders will also increase by making credit available to VISA and Mastercharge credit card holders. Simply print out space for credit card name, number and expiration date. The holder has only to fill in the blanks and sign his name. When you receive the order, you fill out the information on a merchant credit card form and deposit it in the bank. You can open a merchant account for VISA and Mastercharge at most larger banks everywhere.

Sales tax won't be required, except for orders received from within your own state. Be sure to add a statement such as "California residents please add 6% sales tax."

Also within your terms, offer a strong guarantee. You'll find that a solid guarantee will generate many more sales than an offer without a guarantee. You may have a few returns from dissatisified customers. If you do, handle the returns promptly.

ENVELOPE DESIGN

The envelope which encloses your sales brochure should be appealing enough to the eye to make a good impression and to stimulate some interest. You want to avoid having it appear to be "junk mail". You'll want it to be distinguished from other mailing pieces, and most of all, you'll want the prospect to open and read your message rather than tossing it in the trash.

A standard #10 envelope is appropriate for most sales brochures, while a #9 envelope is ideal to enclose with the #10 for your customer to use to mail back his order. Colored paper, instead of white, usually gets more attention, as does two color printing rather than one color, although two color is more expensive.

Often you'll want to write a message across the bottom of your mailer to stimulate some interest as to what is inside. Whatever the case, your mailing piece should be designed in good taste to compliment the message inside.

FOLLOW UP SALES LETTERS

Successful mail order operators who send off sales material in response to inquiries have found that only about 50% of the orders generated result from the initial sales material mailed out. The remainder of the orders are derived from follow-up mailings to inquirers who did not order initially. The prospect who expressed an interest in your product, yet did not order may have set your offer aside or have forgotten to send it in. Whatever the case, he deserves at least a second opportunity to receive the benefits of your product.

Your follow up mailing should stress some of the same points mentioned in your initial letter, but should offer some other benefits not mentioned earlier. The idea is to keep your prospect interested before he cools off.

Often, it may require five or six follow up letters to obtain a sale. Your first follow up should be mailed within two weeks of the original mailing. Intervals for the following mailing can be every thirty days. Be sure to offer a variation with each letter, including a different benefit to be gained from ordering your product.

Follow up mailings should cease before costs reach a higher level than the relative profit from the return on those mailings.

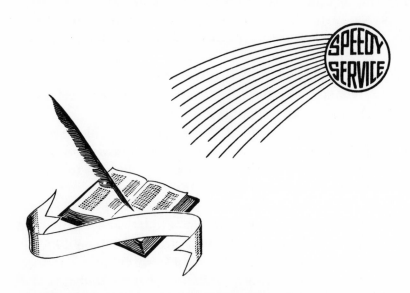

SHIPPING ORDERS & RECORD KEEPING

In this particular phase of your business operation, it is important that you maintain a simple, efficient operation. Plan to ship your products out within one day of receiving an order at the lowest cost and with the least effort. Your customer deserves prompt delivery. When mail order buyers become impatient, they may complain to you directly, or they may make a fuss with postal authorities, the Better Business Bureau, or the publication you advertisied in. To avoid this, send out orders within a day of receiving them. Promoting goodwill among your customers will pay off in repeat orders.

The following are steps necessary to take for handling all incoming mail. These records will determine the profitability and pulling power of each of your advertisements.

1. Separate all mail on a daily basis according to the key symbol delegated to its source, such as all orders from Popular Mechanics in one pile, orders from Playboy in another, etc.

2. On a separate sheet designated for each source, credit each order to the publication or mailing list reponsible for the order. This file sheet should include; name of publication or mailing list, key symbol, a vertical row of the days in the month, a horizontal row of the twelve months, and a tally of the orders next to the day of the month they were received.

3. Remove all checks, money orders, and credit card orders from the envelopes. Place all checks and money orders in one pile and credit card orders in another pile. Stamp all checks and money orders with a rubber stamp denoting "For deposit only" to your checking account. Credit card orders will be processed separately and put into a separate checking account.

4. After all remittances have been removed from their envelopes and all orders have been credited to their sources, stack all the order envelopes in one pile, keeping them in order. Take three sheets of self-adhesive labels, with carbon between, and type out the names and addresses of the customers. The original will be attached to the package and mailed to the customer. The duplicate labels can be used for follow-up later to the same clientele.

5. For indirect replies only. If you are advertising for inquiries only, the processing system has a slight variation. After crediting all responses to their sources, you will print the source key symbol of the inquiry on the lower lefthand corner of the return envelope, which is sent with the sales brochure to the enquirer. Then, when the prospect mails back an order in the return

envelope you will know the source of the order from the key symbol.

Striving for efficiency may become difficult as your business grows from infancy. The large mail order houses have the latest processing equipment complimented by sophisticated computers to automate this time consuming phase of the business. As your business grows, you may want to consider hiring someone, or a firm who specializes in mail order processing.

RETAILING YOUR BOOK

Selling your book in the retail marketplace can be a very rewarding adventure; however, it is also a very difficult and time consuming enterprise. I only suggest the retail market for those of you who already have had some success selling your book in the mail order market.

What makes the retail market difficult is the combination of sales and distribution. The large publishing houses have the solution to these problems as they already have large distribution channels set up to pump new titles into. Sales demand is usually derived from plenty of money spent in the media to make the public aware of a particular title.

But what about you? Assume you have an excellent cookbook which already has sold well through the mail, or a valuable book on gambling which you have a good feeling could sell well nationally. How do you go about getting this fine book of yours into the bookstore?

You could begin by visiting the bookstores in your area to see if the manager of the stores will buy them, usually for 60% of your gross selling price. Often, a bookstore may require you to leave your books on consignment, which means you will be paid for your books once the store sells them.

After you have placed your books on consignment in various stores in the area, go back personally to every store at thirty-day intervals and note the number of books that have sold. Keep a separate accounting of the number of books sold at each store. Later you will use this information to prove to other stores that your book sells. Once you've established a good sales record with your book, it will be easier for you to go off consignment and sell directly to the stores.

Since it is a very basic requirement to have a proven sales background in the retail book business, you cannot go any further at the retail level until you have monitored your book sales in a few local test stores. Eventually you will want to sell your books to large chains of bookstores, publisher representatives, distributors, and individual bookstores throughout the country. Unless you are a famous writer or have a proven sales record, these large wholesale buyers of books won't consider your book for purchase.

I found this to be true when I sent my first title to the paperback book buyer of Waldenbooks, a chain of 500 stores throughout the United States. They scrutinized my first book very carefully, then purchased a few hundred copies for a select group of stores, only because my book had sold already at a few Walden test stores. Fortunately, the first order sold very well and Walden's placed a second order for 3,000 books for all 500 stores. Six months later, I sent Walden's my second title. They took a quick look at it, briefly skimmed the contents, and placed an order for 2,000 copies immediately. Getting the second order was easy because they now considered me an established author since my first title was already successfully selling in their chain of stores.

Now, with my third title not yet in print, they are already interested in it and have placed an order for the first printing.

OK, let's assume you have monitored your book sales at various stores and it appears to be selling. Your next step is to attempt to get your book in as many stores as possible. Begin by mailing complimentary review copies to the chain store buyers along with a record of your sales in the test stores. Start with Waldenbooks in Stamford Connecticut, B. Dalton Pickwick Booksellers in Minneapolis, and Brentanos and Doubleday in New York City. These companies are the largest in the business and you might as well start by dealing with the largest volume buyers.

Besides the large chains of bookstores, you'll need to sell your book to wholesale book distributors and publisher representatives in order to widely distribute your title. Wholesale book distributors operate by warehousing thousands of titles, which allow book stores to centralize their book purchasing. Book wholesalers offer the stores a discount of 25 to over 40% off the retail price, depending on the quantities ordered, and usually charge the store for shipping. In turn, the book wholesaler requires a 50% discount from the publisher in order to operate and still make a profit.

Publisher representatives operate differently from wholesale distributors, although they often distribute books themselves, their basic function is to represent complete lines of books from various publishers, making personal calls directly to bookstores. Since they function in more of a sales capacity then do distributors, they require a commission of 5 to 10% for their services. You can locate publisher reps either by asking your local bookstore for the name of good reps, or by looking in the Yellow

Pages under publisher representatives.

Just like the mail order business, the retail book business requires a good guarantee in order to sell effectively. In the retail book business it is referred to as return privileges. If the stores or distributors buy your books, full return privileges entitle them to return your books for a full refund, or credit for another title you may have selling if your books do not sell over an extended period. Usually, this priviliege is offered by publisheres and last six months from the date the book was placed on the shelf for sale. Without a good return policy it is very difficult for a new publisher to sell effectively.

When I first entered the book business a few years ago, I was confronted with the problem of distribution. I found that I had a couple of good saleable titles, but how was I to get them into the 30,000 book outlets throughout the country? Then I started traveling throughout the country selling books store to store, sometimes even while I was on vacation. Now, after three years, my books are in some 1200 American stores, plus 150 in Canada. I have still to conquer the other 28,000 plus stores, but I will someday. Probably through the mail.

While I was selling my first title three years ago in southern California, I met an elderly gentleman by the name of Marvin Lindeman, who happened to be talking to a bookstore manager while I was in the same store. I asked him a few questions and was amazed at what he was doing. He had four titles he had written, from "Breakthrough in Blackjack" to "How to Buy Income Property." He and his wife would attach a travel-trailer to the back of his car and drive throughout the country selling all four titles to individual bookstores. He had been retired for quite sometime and found that selling his books door-to-door while traveling not only paid his traveling expenses, but also became quite a lucrative business.

Now, I seem to see Marvin Lindeman's books in just about every bookstore I enter. And I envy him; although often I do the same thing myself, it's a great life, especially if you like to travel.

THE ULTIMATE IN SUCCESS

Once you have developed your direct reply business into a thriving enterprise, and your profits are substantial enough that you can begin considering where to invest them, you'll basically have two choices: either put your profits back into your existing business, or invest them elsewhere. You could choose a third alternative of spending the proftis on vacations, fancy cars, etc, but that wouldn't fit within our framework of acquiring the financial independence you are planning to attain.

When considering putting your profits back into your business, remember the basic ingredients for success are low overhead coupled with increasing sales of a good product. Use your money wisely to increase sales without adding to overhead costs.

If you prefer to invest your profits elsewhere, my obvious preference is in residential real estate. The advantages of investing in real estate are almost unlimited, as I have stated earlier in Book I. The ultimate success for you will be to begin investing your proceeds into various forms of real estate while still operating your mail order business.

The biggst advantage you have in owning real estate is that your real estate investments literally make money while you sleep. Although your direct reply business will, in most cases, be very successful. The real estate investments derived from the profits of your mail order business, on the other hand, will continue to appreciate as time goes on.

Personally, I look at my own direct reply business simply as a source of income which I invest in real estate. Since I feel that becoming the ultimate landlord, with oodles of property, is the best and most secure way to become financially independent. In other words, my mail order business is merely a means to an end...that of acquiring enough real estate to be independently wealthy enough never to have to work again. I do enjoy operating my mail order business very much; however it continues to require constant care and attention. My idea of the ideal life is working when and where I want, about six months a year, with vacation and travel occupying the remainder of my time. Owning plenty of real estate is the only way I know to remain free to do what I want. And, the best way I know to acquire plenty of real estate is to develop a prospering direct reply business in order to get the excess capital to buy that real estate.

It is truly a wonderful feeling to enjoy the freedom financial independence can bring. With the conclusion of this book, I hope I've widened some horizons and have given you some insight towards the financial security you deserve.

Whatever level of achievement you attain while working at the two enterprises I've introduced to you...I sincerely wish you the best in your quest for success.

Another book by ANDREW JAMES McLEAN
THE POWER OF REAL ESTATE
and how to acquire it in your spare time.

"The greatest condensed guidebook to investing in real estate ever written."

-Writers Post

Please note that although this book, The Power of Real Estate, is written differently and includes other topics of interest, it is similar in content to Book I of The Power of Financial Independence. It does however feature investing in foreclosure property.

Available at popular bookstores everywhere. Or, order direct from the publisher. Send $4.95 plus 60¢ postage and handling to JWP Development, PO Box 2531, Culver City, CA, 90230.